In The Land Of
Hummel

In The Land Of
Hummel

Traditional Bavarian Life

Photographs by Walter Pfeiffer

Text by Kathleen Saal

A Robert Campbell Rowe Book
Portfolio Press

Library of Congress Catalog Card
Number 99-74557

ISBN 0-9242620-28-3

All inquiries regarding this book
should be addressed to:
Portfolio Press, 130 Wineow Street,
Cumberland, Maryland 21502.

Project Editor:
Krystyna Poray Goddu

Designed by
John Vanden-Heuvel Design

Printed and bound by
New Interlitho Italia, Milan, Italy

Contents

Prologue   14

Introduction   20

Part 1: Autumn   26

The First Day in Bavaria   28

A Bavarian Home   30

Daily Life in the Countryside   34

Berta Hummel's Homeland   40

The Blacksmith   44

Almabtrieb   46

Painting Wooden Handicrafts   48

Giving Thanks   50

Gamsbart   52

Bells and the Bell Foundry   54

Leonhardiritt   58

Part 2: Winter   60

Christkindlmarkt   62

Saint Nikolaus Day   66

The Wooden Crèche Tradition   68

The Hummel Nativity Set   72

Christmas   74

The Chimney Sweep   80

Contents

New Year's Eve and Epiphany   82

Crafting Hummel Figurines   84

Fasching   90

Part 3: Spring   94

The Barrel Maker   96

Munich   98

Trachten   100

Bamberg   108

Sister Maria Innocentia's Tale Unfolds   112

Easter   114

Maypoles   116

The Wagon-Wheel Maker   120

Pilgrimages   122

Part 4: Summer   128

In a Bavarian Beer Garden   130

Embroidered Masterpieces   134

Rothenburg ob der Tauber   136

Lüftlmalerei   140

The Shepherd   144

The Siessen Convent   146

Museums of Bavarian Culture   156

Acknowledgements   158

Index to Hummel figurines   160

Prologue

THIS STORY BEGINS WITH A SIMPLE childhood request, one I would repeat with eager anticipation every time I saw my grandmother.

"Tell me a story about when you were a little girl in Bavaria."

As a child growing up in middle America, I would sit spellbound in my grandmother's lap for hours, listening to the stories of her Bavarian youth. They were about people I had never met and faraway places I had never seen, but her colorful words and recollections about this place she called *Bayern* came to life in my young and lively imagination.

Bavaria's captivating scenery ranges from mountains and meadows to medieval settings. Burghausen, right, has Europe's longest castle.

To me, my grandmother's stories were as vivid and exciting as anything I could find in a book of fairy tales. After all, she, too, spoke of kings and castles, medieval towns and ancient walled cities. She would lace her descriptions with such exacting detail that it seemed as if I could actually see the places she spoke of—the breathtaking mountain vistas speckled with tiny wooden huts and wandering sheep or cows, the landscapes of tall ever-

greens, lush green meadows and heaven-caressing hills, and the timbered houses that burst into full bloom from one window to the next.

Still, the tales I loved best were the ones she would tell about everyday life in Bavaria. The land of my grandmother's youth was a place where people wore clothes that had unusual names— *Lederhosen* were leather pants, while a *Dirndl* was the name of the dress my grandmother wore, and, my favorite, the *Gamsbart*, was something that looked surprisingly like my grandfather's shaving brush, except people wore it upside down on their hats! Religion, too, was an ever-present part of everyday life, from the statues and pictures reverently displayed in rooms at home to the devotional wayside shrines dotting the countryside and the countless church holidays celebrated each year with parades, festive costumes and solemn pageantry. And in the warmer months, there were special countryside festivals, called *Volksfeste*, where you could find irresistible treats like sugar-coated, roasted nuts, soft, salty pretzels and big gingerbread hearts with strings attached so you could wear them like a necklace. Sometimes, at extra-special events, there was even a beau-

16

tifully painted musical carousel, swings and other amusements for the children. The grown-ups would usually find their entertainment at long wooden tables, where they'd eat, laugh, sing songs, and drink beer that was poured from giant wooden barrels into tall, heavy mugs.

It was a simpler place in a simpler time, when everyday items like toys and furniture, linens, clothes, and even the houses they were kept in, were carefully and patiently crafted by hand. I would listen dreamily as my grandmother described the cozy duvets under which she snuggled on cold and wintry nights, and the embroidered linens and wax figurines kept by her mother in an armoire lovingly decorated with hand-painted motifs and designs. Her Bavaria was also a land of tempting tastes and aromas, from the fragrant round

The hand-painted motifs and designs on traditional Bavarian furnishings, such as those above, are specific to the region in which they are crafted.

loaves of fresh baked dark bread, to the sweet, creamy homemade butter and the seemingly endless variety of delicious dumplings, sausages, and smoked meats.

The best time of all was at Christmas, when my grandmother would sing or hum perennial favorites like *"Stille Nacht, Heilige Nacht," "O, Tannenbaum,"* and *"Kling, Glöckchen"* as we busied ourselves in the kitchen. We would bake all sorts of delectable delights with exotic names, like *Springerle*, with their delicate designs

pressed from old wooden molds. There was the fragile *Spekulatius*, spicy *Pfefferkuchen*, hazelnut-accented *Magenspitz*, crescent-shaped *Vanillekipferl*, and, one of my favorites, frosted, cinnamony *Zimtsterne*. Today the appealing aromas of cloves, brown sugar, aniseed and vanilla always bring back fond memories of those merry and wonderful moments with my grandmother.

I always wanted to know more. And she was always willing to oblige.

It was when I was nine or ten years old and visiting my best friend from school, that I caught my first glimpse of Hummel figurines.

"What are these?" I asked, pointing to the carefully assembled collection of rosy-cheeked ceramic children, who seemed to be curiously peeking at me from inside a china cabinet. "Those? Oh, they're just my mom's," she replied, "my dad got them for her when he was stationed in Germany with the Army." That's strange, I thought as I looked into the cabinet again, my grandmother had never mentioned anything about them. My curiosity piqued, I later asked my friend's mother to tell me more about these mysterious children, so she took one of the delicate figurines out of the cabinet, gently placed it in my hands and began to tell me about a Franciscan nun who had lived in Germany earlier in this century—her name was Sister Maria Innocentia Hummel.

"Who was she?" I asked, "and who were these children? Were they real people like me?" These handcrafted creations, I was told, were based on the artwork of Sister Maria Innocentia, the former Berta Hummel, who loved to sketch, draw and paint children, often taking her inspiration from the children who lived near her convent, as well as from her own happy childhood. I learned that Sister Maria Innocentia was born, like my grandmother, in the rural countryside of Bavaria. The two were close in age, and, I guessed, would have had similar childhood experiences, so it was with continual wonder that I admired those enchanting Hummel figurines, imagining that they were figures of my grandmother as a child in Bavaria.

My interest in my grandmother's homeland never diminished. My hunger for more stories remained with me for years, finally bringing me to Bavaria for a year abroad after college graduation. I wanted to see for myself this colorful land of my ancestors, the place that I had heard so much about, which had existed, for me, solely in my imagination. The Bavaria I found in the 1990s was a vastly more modern country than the one in which my grandmother had lived earlier in this century and yet, as I discovered over the course of my unforgettable year, the best of Bavaria's past is still very much alive.

The handcrafted porcelain Hummel figurines evoke a traditional Bavarian childhood. Above: HUM 8, Book Worm; *below:* HUM 142, Apple Tree Boy; *opposite page:* HUM 387, Valentine Gift.

Introduction

GOTT MIT DIR DU LAND DER BAYERN...” These seven German words, loosely translated as “God be with you, Bavaria,” begin the Bavarian National anthem, a romantically worded song which today is still sung and played with immense pride. These opening words reveal much about Bavaria and the Bavarians themselves, and are perhaps symbolic of the strong relationship between the picturesque land and its people, who throughout the ages have remained proud, individualistic, tradition-bound and deeply God-loving and God-fearing—both in pagan and Christian times.

With almost prayer-like lyrics, the anthem asks God to protect Bavaria, its fields and villages, and to unite the people of the land from the Alps to the Main. And with a bit of characteristic Bavarian sass, it also requests that God allow the skies above to remain white and blue—a not-too-modest plea since these are the same hues as the national colors of Bavaria.

The gentle settings of Freistaat Bayern (*the Free State of Bavaria*) *belie the region's fiercely independent mind-set.*

It may appear otherwise, but Bavaria is a constituent part of the Federal Republic of Germany. In fact, it is the largest of the country's sixteen states. But Bavaria, a politically conservative and largely Roman Catholic state in a somewhat liberal and mainly Protestant Germany, has never quite relinquished its bold and fiercely independent mind-set. It may be surprising for some to learn that Bavaria still has not ratified the 1949 constitution that made it an official part of the Federal Republic of Germany.

It is no surprise to the Bavarians. Regional lore has it

that the word *bairisch*, or Bavarian, existed long before the word for German—*Deutsche*. This is but a small indication of how Bavaria and the Bavarians view their place in the world. Collectively, the national anthem, the national colors and the oft-seen words *"Freistaat Bayern,"* meaning the Free State of Bavaria, are perhaps the most visible evidence of a long-held and deeply cherished Bavarian ideal.

Originally, the historic region of *Altbayern*, or Old Bavaria, encompassed wide stretches of land near the ancient towns of Freising, Landshut and Regensburg. At one point in history, this region even extended so far south as to include a large portion of modern-day Austria and the region of northern Italy known as South Tyrol. The Bavaria of today is still far-reaching, covering more than 70,000 square kilometers. While it has a modern, industrially dominated and tourism-influenced economy, a full eighty percent of the land mass is devoted to agriculture or foresta-

tion. Bavaria is a vastness that is marked throughout by an assortment of stark contrasts.

Within Bavaria itself there are four—some break it into seven—distinctly different regions, the best known of which, perhaps, is *München-Oberbayern*, home not only to the courtly elegance of the former Wittelsbach rulers and an array of monastic architectural jewels, but also loved for the gentle romance of innumerable lakes in the *Voralpenland* (Alpine Foreland) and the Bavarian Alps with their picture-perfect villages, onion-shaped Byzantine church steeples and awe-inspiring peaks. Even the Bavarian capital, Munich, with all of its multicultural and artistic riches, feels equally comfortable in a savvy high-tech business suit or the *Lederhosen*-clad craziness of the ever-popular *Oktoberfest*.

The airy, impressive elevations and spacious stretches of *Allgäu-Bayerisch Schwaben* in the southwest region of Bavaria are home to the storybook castle of Neuschwanstein as well as to a variety of tempting favorite foods, including hand-made mountain cheeses, exquisite chocolates and *Spätzle* noodles. From the Allgäu Alps northward, the environs cradle the southern end of the famed Romantic Road, which winds its way through a wealth of landscaped and timeless history—from the picturesque Forggen Lake near Schwangau to Roman-founded Augsburg and the ancient walled town of Nördlingen im Ries.

Majestic alpine vistas, romantic castles and monastic architectural jewels, like Kloster Ettal, below, are scenic treasures.

The timeless allure of *Franken*, at Bavaria's northern border,

is due to its intriguing mixture of baroque and rococo accents; its medieval towns in subdued, earthen tones; its elevated fortresses, the characteristic *Fachwerk*, or half-timbered, houses; and its sun-drenched vineyards, which line the winding rivers Main and Tauber. The region, known also for its wine cellars and beer cellars and its sauerkraut and potatoes, is sometimes divided further into the three administrative areas of *Mittelfranken*, *Oberfranken* and *Unterfranken*. Lastly, the pastured lowlands of *Niederbayern* (Lower Bavaria) with their colorful patchwork fields of corn, barley, rye, wheat, oats, sugar beets and canola, and the wooded, sparsely populated scenery of *Oberpfalz* (Upper Palatinate), characterized by Jurassic period rocks, gentle rolling hills and quiet valleys, make up the region known as *Ostbayern* (east Bavaria). *Ostbayern* counts among its celebrated Bavarian neighbors the famed *Hallertau* hops-growing region, and among its more notable inhabitants the mighty Danube, meandering its way eastwards toward Austria.

The timeless allure of Franken, *opposite page, lies in its characteristic half-timbered houses. The rolling hills below are near Markt Schellenberg.*

Viewed in its entirety, Bavaria is a land of amazing and extensive diversity, captivating backdrops and pleasing old-world charm, not only for the multitudes of international tourists who visit each year, but also for legions of inquisitive Germans, many of whom look upon the region as a foreign country in their own backyard. "Why," they'll exclaim, "the Bavarians don't even speak German!"

It's true—no dictionary and certainly no language course

quite prepared me for Bavaria's unique vocabulary and sometimes puzzling dialects, which vary from region to region and village to village. But perhaps that is part of the intrigue and allure of this fascinating land.

The lighthearted and good-natured Bavarian folk have a dialectical saying that goes *"Mir san mir"*—that's *"Wir sind wir"* in *Hochdeutsch* (standard German) or in English: "We are who we are." It is their way of saying, "We know we are different, but that is what makes us special. Please accept us for who we are."

Let me tell you about Bavaria and the Bavarians, as seen through my ever-exploring eyes. Here is Bavaria's story and mine.

AUTUMN

The First Day In Bavaria

I AWOKE THE FIRST MORNING TO ONE of the most glorious sounds I have ever heard. As the pre-autumn sun started to peek through a window, illuminating for the first time the rich textures of my bedroom, the bells of the nearby village church began to peal in unison, announcing, with a rather determined glee, the start of a new day. As I lay in bed, my eyes still heavy with sleep, I imagined that those bells were also announcing my long-anticipated arrival in this almost dream-like land. Slowly, I began to realize that this was not a dream, and that I was actually, at long last, here in Bavaria.

The flight to Munich had seemed excruciatingly long and tiring, but this, no doubt, had more to do with my sleepless excitement than anything else. My host family, the Hoffmanns, an affable and hearty couple with five grown children, two of whom still live at home, have a midsized farm, with an assorted collection of horses, cows, geese and chickens, in a small, unassuming village that is part of the pastoral setting near the Bavarian capital. They provided me with an upstairs room of my own for the duration of my visit, and, at first glance, it appeared exactly like the bedrooms my grandmother used to describe: sparsely decorated, yet exceedingly comfortable, with a definite touch of rustic Bavarian charm.

Bursts of colorful floral accents, left, and serene, pastoral landscapes, above, are among the dreamy details of the Bavarian countryside.

The sturdy bed, made of a dark-grained and weathered wood, had exquisite designs with smooth, rounded edges ornately carved into both the head- and footboards, panels of which were further highlighted with traditional motifs in brilliant and carefully painted brush strokes. The bed itself was covered with a cool, freshly pressed sheet, a large dreamy pillow and an invitingly warm and comfy goose-down duvet, the likes of which I've never seen

before. Fluffed up thick and high, it seemed more like a landlocked cloud than a mere bedcover!

Next to the bed was a simple wooden table, with a candle and a small German prayer book, upon

which someone had welcomingly placed a bouquet of wildflowers—these must have been picked in the meadow behind the farmhouse just prior to my arrival. The wooden floor was worn from years of use, but still smooth and immaculate in appearance, and bedecked with several roughly woven and uniquely patterned cotton rugs. Standing against the wall, with a rather imposing presence, was a sizable armoire—what they call a *Bauernschrank*—which, like the bed, was decorated with striking accents and detailed regional designs. It was a regal, if temporary, quarters for my noticeably American wardrobe over the coming months.

A Bavarian Home

"OH, IF HOUSES COULD ONLY SPEAK!" THIS was the prevailing thought crossing my mind as I wandered through the Hoffmanns' farmhouse, acquainting myself with my marvelously new, yet somehow strangely familiar, surroundings. The curtained windows, the intriguingly different furniture, the old sewing machine, the pleasant home-cooked aromas—it seemed that all of these things were conspiring to finally bring to life those tales my grandmother shared with me so long ago.

My grandmother's Bavaria was a simpler place in a simpler time.
Right: HUM 390, Boy with Accordion; HUM 150, Happy Days.

"*The Stube,*" I could hear her say, "was the focal point and, undeniably, the most important room in our house. It was the center of our family life, the place we would gather for meals and celebrations, to work, sew, and even to welcome visiting relatives and neighbors, sometimes passing the night away with card games or singing traditional folk melodies. My *Opa* (grandfather) played the accordion while my uncle Georg joined in on the

fiddle and my father played the zither."

The *Stube* was always the brightest and most inviting area of the house, thanks to its intentional southern exposure and the large windows built into the two corner walls to capture the brightness and warmth of the sun as it made its daily dash across the skies.

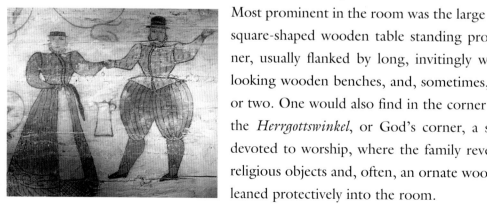

Most prominent in the room was the large square-shaped wooden table standing proudly in the corner, usually flanked by long, invitingly wide and friendly looking wooden benches, and, sometimes, a wooden chair or two. One would also find in the corner above the table, the *Herrgottswinkel*, or God's corner, a space specifically devoted to worship, where the family reverently displayed religious objects and, often, an ornate wooden crucifix that leaned protectively into the room.

An inviting Stube, *above, includes the traditional* Herrgottswinkel. *A seventeenth-century painted bedroom mural, below left, depicts scenes of daily life.*

"My father would always sit at that table with a broad, jolly smile, slowly twisting the upward-turning curls of his mustache between his finger and thumb," my grandmother would reminisce. "In front of him sat a tall stoneware mug filled with beer, bottles of which my brothers Sepp and Andreas had brought home earlier in the day from the proprietor of the nearby *Gasthaus*

(inn). Every so often, and usually it was during long, cold wintry nights, after they had spent a strenuous day working around the farm, cleaning the stalls, feeding the pigs, caring for the horses, and cutting firewood, I'd find my father and my *Opa* sitting in this cozy, candlelit room silently carving pieces of wood. They told me it helped them relax and pass the time."

The armoire of a new bride, below, was customarily filled with bundles of spun flax, linens, cords of beeswax and special votives.

Of equal importance in many Bavarian households was the tiled *Kachelofen*, or heating stove, which sat in the *Stube* opposite the table. Often encircled by a sitting bench, it was physically connected, through a common wall with the kitchen, to the wood-burning cooking stove. The marvel of this unique duo, a variation of which is still used today in many Bavarian houses and homey, traditional restaurants and inns, was that it served two critical purposes—cooking and heating—so the kitchen and the *Stube* were, in effect, the only truly heated rooms in the house.

"On cold, rainy days, my brothers and sisters and I would run home after school,

and as soon as we entered the dry, toasty *Stube*, we'd hang our clothes above the *Kachelofen* to dry," my grandmother would say wistfully, adding, "we loved to sit there next to that tiled, cozy warmth, chasing the chill away. Our mother was usually busy with chores around the farm, but sometimes we'd find her, along with our grandmother—we called her *Oma*—in the kitchen, making butter, preserving fruits and vegetables from the garden or preparing a meal, like soup and dumplings. It took some encouraging, but sometimes we could convince *Oma* to join us for a little while in the *Stube*. While she sat next to that comfortable warmth, she would quietly mend some of our worn clothes or knit."

Daily Life In The Countryside

A S A CHILD, I USED TO THINK THAT all the houses in Bavaria were sculpted out of gingerbread and white icing, with stained-glass windows of melted lollipops, candy cane-accented doors, and an orderly row of colorful gumdrop bushes outside. As I walked around, admiring these carefully designed dwellings in the Hoffmanns' village, I realized that my fabled visions were not entirely correct—but they were not altogether wrong. Although made from materials definitely less tempting to a sweet tooth, the houses were assembled with exceptional craftsmanship and delightful storybook touches, from the protectively wide roofs covered with patterned, red clay tiles or carefully laid wooden shingles to the carved wooden trim and window shutters and the

An invitingly large wooden bench, opposite page, top, is the perfect place to pass some time on a sunny afternoon in the countryside. Right: HUM 112, Just Resting.

charming wooden balconies, preened with eye-catching motifs and cutout designs of such exactness that they appeared to have been made with a cookie cutter.

"And what about the flowers, I can't forget those," I exclaimed out loud, gazing at the vast and varied explosions of cheerful color that seemed to sprout up from balconies, windows, and gardens.

The elaborate displays of cascading geraniums and other radiant blooms burst from the surroundings like vibrant paints on a canvas.

Farmhouses, in particular, are still found in traditional layouts of one-to-four large buildings, depending on the size and regional location of the farm. The living quarters and the stables, or stalls, are under the same roof, which may look unusual to an American,

In Alpine areas, heavy stones were placed atop wooden shingles, as above, to prevent them from flying away in high winds.

but is, for the Bavarian farmer, a very practical design. A large interior barnyard is the noticeable feature of the larger *Dreiseithof*, or three-sided farm, where the buildings are set out in a "C" shape, and the *Vierseithof*, a four-

Everyone, old and young, is expected to do their share of work around the farm. Below, from left: HUM 321, Wash Day; HUM 73, Little Helper; HUM 171, Little Sweeper; HUM 363, Big Housecleaning; HUM 74, Little Gardener.

sided seemingly enclosed structure, like the Hoffmanns', that, to me, looked almost like a fortified farmer's castle.

It was interesting to see that the wooden houses and barns so common at the start of this century were assembled much like an intricate,

three-dimensional puzzle, each piece fitting exactly into another through the use of precisely shaped wooden boards, logs, joints and pegs, some carved into imaginative and whimsical shapes. In the alpine areas, large, heavy stones were typically placed atop the shingled roofs to ensure that the sheltering wooden planks didn't blow away in a storm.

It was a harder and far more self-sufficient existence. I remember my grandmother telling me that everyone was expected to do their share of work around the farm, even the grandparents and the young children. "My brothers had to work long hours in the fields with our father," she said, "and my sisters and I, we helped our mother, whether it was the time-consuming chore of washing clothes by hand, working in the garden or taking care of the chickens and geese. Many farmers also had hired hands—called *Mägde* (maidens) and *Knechte* (farm laborers). The *Mägde*, typically, were responsible for the milk cows and the pigs, while the *Knechte* would care for the

horses and oxen." Families had suitably sized gardens for growing vegetables to feed all the members, and there were usually fruit trees, too, bearing apples, pears, cherries or plums. The absolute necessity of every day life, however, was bread—whether plain or spread with butter or *Schmalz* (lard).

"Many people," my grandmother often reminded me, "did not have the convenience of living near a bakery," so they had to bake bread themselves, and this was usually done in a small free-standing *Backhaus*, a baking house, which was kept separate from the living quarters because of the danger of fire. "We had a baking day about every ten days, and my mother, grandmother, sisters and I would wake up early so that we could make the best use of the daylight hours. After all, it

In autumn, fruit trees yield a bountiful supply of colorful and tasty apples, pears and plums. Left: HUM 199, Feeding Time.

38

wasn't like we could turn a knob and ten minutes later the oven was heated and ready! My mother always prepared the yeasty sourdough starter the night before to allow it time to rise. Our job then was to mix and knead this with the flour and other ingredients by hand—not just for one *Laib* (loaf), but for as many as two dozen loaves of bread! And before putting any

of the loaves into the oven, we had to stoke the wood fire, letting it burn for a whole hour before the heat was just right. Only then could we begin our baking. It was a lot of work, but the treat for me was always that wonderful aroma. Sometimes my brothers, lured away from their chores, would trick my grandmother and sneak off with a warm, freshly baked loaf. I usually found them later in the

*A traditional hay wagon, above, and beehives, like the one at left, were common sights in rural farming areas.
Below: HUM 312, Honey Lover.*

orchard, sitting under an apple tree, savoring slices of bread that were slathered with fresh butter."

Sweet, golden, delectable honey was also a part of the Bavarian diet, and for a long time the only substance available for sweetening food and drinks. "A day without honey," my grandmother would always say, "is like a day without sunshine." Beehives were kept either directly outside the house, on a balcony or under the roof, or in the orchard, when one existed. The wisdom of keeping a *Bienenhaus* was three-fold, enabling not only the production of that luscious liquid sunshine, but also the pollination of one's fruit trees in spring, and the collection of an important byproduct, beeswax, which was used to make special religious votives, and often even donated to the church.

Berta Hummel's Homeland

THEY CALL IT A BAYERISCHER HIMMEL, or Bavarian heaven, when the skies above are painted in a clear and vibrant blue dotted sparingly with puffy, cotton-white clouds, and it was on such a magnificent day that I set out to see some of the countryside. As I gazed hypnotically at the changing scenery outside the window of a train, a kindly old woman, who had sat down next to me a short while earlier, struck up a conversation. My ears perked up when she mentioned that it was in placid, rural surroundings like these that the young Berta Hummel had spent her childhood. My attention pulled away from the sights outside, I turned my head toward her and listened more closely. "Berta was born the same year as

Berta Hummel was born in 1909 in the town of Massing, situated on the Rott river. The town today, below, is still a peaceful one.

one of my sisters, 1909 it was, in a town on the Rott river called Massing. That's here in *Niederbayern*," she said proudly, "and it's not far from where I grew up, the youngest of eight children. Bertl—that's how she was often called in the Bavarian dialect—also came from a large family, having three sisters and two brothers."

"Back in those days," the woman continued, "Massing was sort of a center of commerce, and often, on market days especially, my father, grandfather, and uncles, like most of the farmers in the area, would dress up in their best *Trachten* (folk costumes), hitch their horses to their wagons, and ride into town to sell their goods. Berta's father, Adolf Hummel, was a well-known merchant who owned a general store in Massing—a family business inherited from his father, Jakob

Hummel. My mother always said that store, with its wide selection of household notions, textiles, foodstuffs and tools, was one of the finest around. It was there, in front of the store, on the market square, that the farmers gathered, always making time to discuss the latest goings on and share some laughs before going their separate ways. My brothers and sisters and I always looked forward to those days because our father would return home with a special treat of freshly baked, salty *Brezen* (pretzels)."

I had savored every word this woman had spoken, and now asked her, hopefully, "Did you know Berta yourself?" She paused a moment, as if deep in thought, and then responded, "No, not personally. I was too young," she explained, "but I knew of her through one of my sisters. They both went to Marienhöhe, a boarding school for girls, which was run by the Institute of English Sisters, not far from Massing, in a town called Simbach, on the Inn river. I remember my sister saying Berta, who was popular among her schoolmates, was a talented artist, even at that early age. One time she even brought home a sketch that Berta had made of her. She was very proud of it." The train began slowing to a halt at the next station and the old woman gathered her belongings, bidding me a cheerful Bavarian *"Pfüagod"* as she departed. Yes, so long, I thought, waving, until the next time we see each other.

The Blacksmith

THE ROOM WAS DARK AND SMOKY WHEN I first entered. In the far corner there was a blazing fire, with interchanging flickers of bright orange, yellow and red. The only sound was a loud, rhythmic "cling, clang; cling, clang" as a man struck a heavy hammer against a rod of hot, glowing iron, causing a shower of fiery sparks to fall to the floor. I was in the workshop of the *Schmied*, what we call a blacksmith, as I had volunteered to pick up something for Herr Hoffmann. This was a selfish offer on my part; I wanted the opportunity to observe for myself this age-old profession, passed down from one generation to the next, because I had learned—through some genealogical research, this time—that one of my German ancestors had been a *Schmied*.

"*Bitt'schön*," the man said in a thick Bavarian dialect, as he looked up at me to offer help.

"I am here to pick up some horseshoes for Herr Hoffmann," I told him, admiring the raw beauty of the door locks and hinges on his workbench. It was hard to believe that these delicate designs, with their clean, rounded edges, were the product of such rugged surroundings. Looking around the dusky room, I noticed an orderly collection of large hammers and an assortment of other tools with very long handles.

"Those handles are to ensure that a blacksmith's hands are a safe distance from the burning hot iron," he explained, noting my all-

too-obvious curiosity. He motioned for me to come closer so that I could see what he was making. As I watched him work, I mentioned why I was in Bavaria and all that I hoped to see during my visit.

"Jeder ist seines Glückes Schmied," he said. Later, I learned from Herr Hoffmann that this idiomatic expression means: everyone should use the chances that life offers them. Deciding that this was especially good advice for the months ahead of me in Bavaria, I jotted the saying down in my journal.

Almabtrieb

When the days are getting shorter and the leaves have started transforming the landscape into a multicolored palette of reds, oranges and yellows, there is, in the Bavarian and Allgäu Alps, a yearly spectacle that is called the *Almabtrieb*, or *Viehscheid*. This is the ritual in which the cows, having spent the warm summer months—the *Alm-sommer*—in higher and decidedly cooler climes, dining on the sweet grasses of their serene mountaintop pastures and producing milk for cheeses and rich, creamy butter, return to the valleys ahead of the first winter snows. If the summer has passed without illness or tragedy befalling the farmer's family and the cows, the animals are festively decorated for the long hike home.

In the Allgäu, this honor is bestowed on the lead cow only, but in the Bavarian Alps, near Berchtesgaden, all of the cows are dressed in a

The elaborate Fuikl *atop this cow's head is a splendid form of folk art unique to the Alpine region near Berchtesgaden. Left:* HUM 334, Homeward Bound.

Fuikl, a specially made crown of fresh-cut evergreen branches, mountain flowers and ribbons in a rainbow of splendid, spirited hues. Each cow is fitted with a distinctively different sounding bell around its neck, so that every forward-moving stride and swing of a magnificent head during the trek down the mountain path produces, in unison, a most memorable clinging and clanging. According to popular

superstition, this symphony of mountain music will ward off any bad spirits in the cows' path. The exact dates of these traditional and colorful parades vary by region and depend largely on the weather at the particular mountain *Alm*, where the *Sennerin*—the milk maid—has spent the summer months, caring for her four-legged charges.

Painting Wooden Handicrafts

Wₕₑₙ young Berta Hummel was at the Marienhöhe in Simbach, she often spent her summer recess at an aunt's house in Berchtesgaden, where she would sketch and paint the captivating mountain scenery. I, too, was taken in by the natural beauty of this enchanting enclave, which is tucked between the magnificent peaks and thick forests of the Alps and the nearby Austrian frontier. The region, I was pleased to find, has a long history of imaginative and uncommon folk art, an off-shoot of an ancient wood handicrafts industry that originated with the making of such household necessities as wooden plates, spoons and butter churns.

A Spanschachtel's designs can take hours to paint. The motif above is called a "Federkiel," because in earlier times it was painted with a feather.

"Please have a seat," the artist said, as she carefully applied the painted features to a platoon of wingless, wooden angels neatly arranged in front of her. Looking around the room, I spotted spindle-shaped wooden dolls, flocks of colorful wooden birds, various miniature figurines of exacting and whimsical detail, wooden spinning tops and toy whistles. It was as though I had stumbled upon a secret work-

shop for Santa Claus! Then I noticed an item that looked surprisingly similar to something I had once seen as a young girl. "What is this?" I asked enthusiastically, pointing at an over-sized, perfectly painted wooden box, one of many, in various shapes and sizes, sitting on the shelf. "It's called a *Spanschachtel,* a form of folk art unique to Berchtesgadener Land," the artist responded.

My grandmother had had a very old *Spanschachtel,* in which she kept some treasured family photos and mementos of her

childhood, I quietly remembered as I
sat, in awe of all the marvelous workmanship in the room. Pausing in her work, the
artist looked up at me again and explained,
"Long ago, pharmacies and spice mer-
chants used these pine boxes to hold their
wares because they were dry and odorless. Now, people use
them for many things, for holding special hats, heirloom
clothes, jewelry or even cookies. Some people buy them
simply for decoration. Each one is carefully and individually crafted by hand from split wood, and then sent here
for us to paint with traditional motifs or designs. Our
long tradition of wooden handicrafts is second only to
salt in being the region's most important export."

Giving Thanks

ROM THE SLOPING HILLS OF *Franken's* vineyards to the well-groomed corn fields of *Niederbayern*, October is, for Bavaria's farming communities, the time to finish the harvest, take stock of the summer that has passed, and make final preparations for the winter and spring that lie ahead. Fields of dried stalks of corn are cut down and

made into silage, sugar beets and potatoes are gathered from their earthy summer homes, apples are picked and sorted, and precious grapes are freed from their leafy dwellings and pressed into vintage wines.

Throughout the countryside,

Franken's vine-yards are planted mainly with white grape varieties. Bratwurst and sauerkraut, below, are among the region's specialities.

this is, above all, the time to give thanks. In Bavaria, there are two separate holidays devoted to expressing gratitude: the *Erntedankfest* on the first Sunday of the month, which is observed with festive church services and sometimes parades and special markets, and, on the third Sunday of the month, *Allerweltskirchweih (Kirta* or *Kirwa* in some regional dialects). The latter is traditionally the day when most of the demanding work of the farmer, in the fields, is finished for the year. This event is distinguished from the separate and more religious *kleiner Kirta*, the dedication day of one's local church, which is also celebrated annually, usually on the feast day of the church's patron saint.

The *Allerweltskirchweih*, or All-Bavarian Sunday fair, is generally a festive occasion of thanksgiving, with a traditional meal of roast goose or duck, but in years gone by, when my grandmother was still a young girl, it had more of a holiday atmosphere, with the food and frolic, the dancing and the laughter lasting for days. There is an old Bavarian saying—*"A richtiga Kirta dauad vom Sunnta bis zum Irta"*—meaning a proper *Kirchweih* doesn't end on Sunday, but continues until Tuesday (*Irta*). My grandmother used to tell me how her mother and grandmother, as well as most other women in their village, would spend the entire Saturday before *Kirchweih*, what was known as *Kirchweihsamstag*, in the kitchen preparing food for the festivities. "The most wonderful smell would spread through our house when they were making *Ausgezogene*, dropping those gently stretched circles of sweet, yeasty dough, one by one, into a pan of hot fat. My brothers and sisters and I could hardly wait to eat them, sprinkled with sugar, or plain," she would remember fondly.

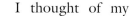

Ausgezogene, *left, with their thin, somewhat moist centers, are a traditional Bavarian treat for* Kirchweih. *Above:* HUM 353, Spring Dance.

I thought of my grandmother as I bit into some fresh *Ausgezogene*, also known as *Fensterkücheln*, *Kücheln* or *Küchle*, now more likely to be sold in bakeries or at farmers' markets than made at home. They look and taste a bit like large, flat doughnuts except, instead of a hole in the middle, there is a thin, somewhat moist center, called the *Fenster* (window), which, if you're lucky, has trapped some of that sprinkled sugar.

51

Gamsbart

EVER SINCE MY CHILDHOOD, I HAD ALWAYS held a certain affection and fascination for the unusually decorative *Gamsbart*. My grandmother used to tell me her uncle wore, tucked into a silver clip on his dark green felt hat, one so big that it looked like a long, wispy brown halo above his head. "Uncle Konrad was a *Berufsjäger*, a professional hunter, who worked in the forest," she would say, occasionally showing me an old, torn photo of her mother's brother, which she kept in her bed-

Originally, a Gamsbart signified the wearer was a hunter, with the tufts of hair worn like a trophy. The longer and thicker the hairs, the better.

room. "He always said that having such a big, round *Gamsbart* was a confirmation of his skills in the mountains." The *Gamsbart* is made of bristly dark tufts of hair from the chamois buck, a goatlike animal native to the Alps. Tufts of a red-tinted deer hair can also be used. The longer the hairs and the more of them that can be bound together, the more trophy-like and valuable the *Gamsbart* becomes.

Bells and the Bell Foundry

I F YOU ARE IN THE COUNTRYSIDE LONG ENOUGH, you begin to notice, as I soon did, something a bit peculiar about the bells in some of the villages and towns. "Why is it," I asked Frau Hoffmann at breakfast one morning, "that in this village, the bells peal so loud and so long at five or six o'clock in the morning and then again at six-thirty in the evening?"

"Back in the days before people wore watches and woke up to an electric alarm clock, they lived, worked and played according to the church bells," she answered. "The bells early in the morning and in the evening, are what we call, in Bavarian, *'Bedleiten'*—a call to prayer.

Before a bell is made, a desired strike tone must be determined, which influences the resulting shape of each bell.

It's not as strictly adhered to today, but when I was a young girl and most certainly when your grandmother was growing up here, these were the times when people woke to start their day and when they had to be back home in the evening, each time reciting a special prayer, called *'Engel des Herrn.'* The bells have other special rings too—to indicate that someone in the village has died, to ward off any approaching bad weather, and to call the farmers in from the fields for lunch."

There were times when I felt as though the marvelously melodic bells had become one of the recurring themes of my travels in Bavaria. It didn't really matter where I

When a mold is dry, it is prepared for the founding process. Removal of the inner fake bell leaves a gap for the heated bronze.

was—city, countryside, even on a hiking trail in the mountains—somewhere off in the distance I could hear them ringing. Sometimes I was not even exactly sure where they were; they could be peeling from the steepled heights of an ancient church, a monastery or a convent, a wayside chapel, or perhaps from the tower of a nearby town hall.

The tradition of the bell foundry, or *Glockengiesserei*, can still be found in the town of Passau, at the confluence of the Danube, Inn and Ilz rivers, where the custom of creating these heavenly sounding, bronze instruments can be traced back to the Middle Ages. Here, the process of casting a bell, whether it weighs twenty pounds or nine tons, is still done according to a centuries'-old family tradition—one that combines knowledgeable creativity with painstakingly precise craftsmanship and weeks of labor-intensive work. At any one time, there can be as many as thirty bells, or more, in the various stages of production, from layering the clay on the massive molds, to drying the molds over hot, glowing embers, to casting the molten copper and tin, allowing it to cool, and, finally, polishing the finished product.

A church steeple can have three-to-four different sized bells, each with five main frequencies in its internal musical scale.
Right: HUM 495, Evening Prayer.

NUR GOTT ALLEIN MEIN HAI I SOLL SEIN

Leonhardiritt

THE AIR WAS COLD AND DAMP WHEN I arrived in Bad Tölz in the predawn hours, eagerly anticipating the spectacle I would see that morning—the *Leonhardiritt*, one of the most popular religious festivities on the calendar of rural Bavaria. The feast of Saint Leonhard (Leonard) falls on November 6th, but is celebrated also on the weekends both before and after this date. The *Leonhardiritt* has, for centuries, been observed with festive pilgrimages and grand processions, mostly through towns and villages, like Bad Tölz, Kreuth, Inchenhofen, Guntersberg, Lippertskirchen and Benediktbeuren,

where Leonhard, a Benedictine abbot, the protector of cattle and the patron saint of horses and their riders, is also the patron of a nearby church or chapel. Riders sit proudly atop their sturdy, well-groomed and festively decorated

Saint Leonhard, the patron saint of horses and their riders, is for young and old alike the "Bayerische Herrgott"—the Bavarian's favorite saint.

horses, with braided manes and tails, while women and children, dressed in their finest, flower-accented folk costumes, sit in dozens of horse-drawn carriages, decorated with garlands. Together they ride to the church or chapel to ask Saint Leonhard's continued blessing on their farms, stalls and stables. The French-born Saint Leonhard is so revered in Bavaria that he is commonly referred to as the *"Bayerische Herrgott"*—the Bavarian's favorite saint.

WINTER

Christkindlmarkt

I F I HAD TO PICK THE TIME OF YEAR I cherish most it would, without a doubt, be the Christmas season, and to be able to spend this joyous time here was, for me, a gift in itself. It was as if the traditions my grandmother so lovingly taught me and the memories she shared had magically come to life, rekindling that bit of childhood innocence and wonder I thought I had lost

long ago. The traditional outdoor Christmas markets, called *Christkindlmarkt* or *Weihnachtsmarkt*, which she so often spoke of, springing to life in the central squares of cities, towns and villages, were more enchanting than I could have ever imagined. Set in freshly fallen snow, the giant lighted Christmas trees, the choirs of singing children and the rows of wooden stalls, deco-

Festive outdoor Christmas markets with rows of wooden stalls can be found around Bavaria beginning the first weekend of Advent.

rated with aromatic limbs of fresh-cut evergreens and filled with handsome wooden nutcracker soldiers, delicate, shiny glass ornaments, handmade candles and the traditional amusing *Zwetschgenmandl* (prune people) created an unforgettable winter scene. This wonderland was enhanced by the delicious smells of grilled sausages, warm spiced wine, and endless varieties of traditional cookies, which looked so much like the ones I baked with my grandmoth-

The architectural splendor of Munich, above and left, provides an eye-catching backdrop to the annual Christkindlmarkt.

er that I had to buy some to find out if they tasted the same too. Yes, I thought, as I savored the spicy taste of *Pfeffernüsse*, the melt-in-your mouth goodness of the *Vanillekipferl* and a sugar-glazed *Lebkuchen*. "They are exactly as I remember," I told the rosy-cheeked woman who had baked them. "I always thought they tasted the best before Christmas!"

Saint Nikolaus Day

LEGENDARY STORIES, CUSTOMS AND TRADITIONS abound surrounding the fourth-century bishop, Saint Nikolaus—the patron saint of sailors and children. On his feast day, December 6th, or, more customarily, after dusk the evening before, children around Europe await his yearly arrival. In Bavaria, Saint Nikolaus usually has a long, white beard and wears bishop's clothing and a tall miter on his head. He carries an ornamental crosier and, most importantly, a large, golden-colored book, in which are recorded the good and bad deeds of all hopeful youngsters. According to custom, Saint Nikolaus visits children and reads what is written about them in his oversized book, then presents them with apples, nuts, mandarin oranges, chocolate and

The feast day of Saint Nikolaus, on December 6th, is eagerly awaited by young and old alike. HUM 2012, St. Nicholas Day.

Lebkuchen from his sack. Those children who don't get a personal visit from Saint Nikolaus find treats from him in sacks, plates or shoes by the front door of the house. Saint Nikolaus, however, does not always travel alone; he often has loud, ugly, frightening companions who, depending on the region of Bavaria, go by the name of *Krampus, Knecht Ruprecht, Rumpelblas, Rauwuckl, Buttmandl, Klaubauf, Buttz, Pelzmärtel* or the *Gangerl*. These dark, forbidding characters are usually covered in fur or straw, and have their origins in pagan rituals aimed at frightening away the demons of a cold, dark winter. Some have scary masks and animal horns, and carry noisy chains, switches or bells. These frightful ogres don't only spook the demons, though, they often terrify children, too!

"When I was about five," the youngest Hoffmann son reminisced one early December evening, "a *Krampus* came to our house with Saint Nikolaus. As Saint Nikolaus read what was recorded in his big book about my older brothers and sisters the *Krampus* whispered to me that if I'd been naughty he'd take his switch to me and carry me away in his burlap sack.

"I was so scared," he remembered, laughing, "that I told my parents I never wanted Saint Nikolaus to come to our house again!"

The Wooden Crèche Tradition

THE HOLY FAMILY AND THE birth of the Christ child are two of the most eternally beloved subjects in art. When expressed in the medium of woodcarving, the faith and beliefs of Christianity take on tangible, three-dimensional form. Germany, and southern Bavaria in particular, has a centuries' long tradition of woodcarvers and wood sculptors, particularly in the towns of Oberammergau and Garmisch-Partenkirchen, where this particular

style of folk art has achieved great notoriety and is still taught in special schools, passed down from one generation to the next.

Oberammergau's tradition in the art of carving and sculpting wood, above and left, can be traced back at least to the tenth century.

Although history credits Saint Francis of Assisi with assembling the first representation of a crèche—in the form that we know today—in the year 1223 in Italy, it is said that the talented artisans of southern Bavaria are largely responsible for exporting the concept of this unique

religious art form to the rest of the world. Crèches—*Weihnachtskrippe* or *Kripperl*—have been created over the years in marble, wax, terracotta, and even painted paper, but one of the most popular media remains wood. There are two principal styles: figurines carved entirely out of wood, in one piece, and those assembled like jointed dolls,

There are two principal styles of crèche figures: those carved entirely out of wood, in one piece, and those assembled like jointed dolls, with carved wooden heads, hands and feet, and dressed in regional or period-specific clothing.

A full day is needed to carve a figurine's head and another to make the hands and feet. This Bavarian artist uses lime wood.

A mixture of chalk and special wood glue provides a surface for painted-on features. A crèche like the one above can take one month to create.

dolls, with carved wooden heads, hands and feet, and dressed in regional or period-specific clothing. The wood used for these figures is painted with a mixture of chalk and a special wood glue, which creates a smooth surface for applying and holding the painted-on color and details.

My first exposure to the Bavarian affinity for collecting, assembling and displaying these elaborate religious scenes came through my grandmother, who had brought several pieces with her when she moved to America, and added a new piece to her collection each year thereafter. Her favorites, she always would say, were the ones carved by her *Opa* on those long, cold winter nights so long ago. "After my *Opa* finished carving them, my *Oma* dressed them in carefully assembled scraps of our old, worn-out clothes, which she had saved and sewn together to look like traditional folk dress," she recalled, stressing, "I didn't have much in the way of toys when I was a child, at least not as elaborate and beautiful as those figurines, so they were a real treasure." And they still are, I thought, as I searched for the perfect piece to add to that heirloom collection this year.

The Hummel Nativity Set

Based upon the art of Sister Maria Innocentia Hummel, and inspired by both her faith and the Bavarian wooden crèche, this porcelain nativity set is part of the tradition of this unique religious art form. The porcelain figures of the Holy Family and the worshippers are framed by a wooden stable.

HUM 214, eleven-piece Nativity Set with wooden stable and HUM 366, Flying Angel.

Christmas

THERE IS SOMETHING ABOUT A BLANKET of new snow that can change your whole perspective of a place, transforming a dark and dreary landscape into a winter scene of spectacular beauty. This was nature's gift on *Heilig Abend*, Christmas Eve, which I celebrated with the Hoffmanns. According to tradition, the Christmas tree is put up and decorated on this day and, after the magic hour of six o'clock, gifts are exchanged. "That was when the Christkindl came," my grandmother used to tell me. "She looked like a beautiful angel and she would ring a bell to let us know that Christmas had arrived. I would run downstairs and into the *Stube* with my brothers and sisters. Once there, I could never take my eyes off the Christmas tree, standing so proudly, lit up like a shimmering star by a dozen or so little candles. It was decorated with apples, nuts, straw stars, wax figurines, cookies and other homemade baubles, as well as a shimmering glass ornament or two. You can hardly imagine what it was to behold such beauty, in the middle of a cold, dark, December winter." I share my grandmother's fascination with the Christmas tree; it is something I have never outgrown.

Cookies like crescent-shaped Vanillekipferl, *frosted* Zimtsterne *and spicy* Pfeffernüsse, *above, are traditional Christmas favorites.*

On Christmas morning, Frau Hoffmann said she wanted to show me one of her special holiday keepsakes. She took something carefully from a wooden cabinet and I could see, as she approached me with it, that she held an old book. "This was a Christmas gift I received when I was a young child," she said, holding it out to me. I guessed that it had been a cherished volume, because the book's jacket was worn and tattered. It wasn't until she set the book on the table in front of me and I began turning the fragile pages,

74

however, that I realized it was a children's book filled with colorful illustrations by Sister Maria Innocentia Hummel. The illustrations were of religious figures as well as of those endearing children like Hansel and Gretel, the *Geigerlein* (Little Fiddler) and *Wanderbub* (Merry Wanderer), which I had seen as porcelain figurines so long ago in my childhood friend's home.

"This is an original copy of *Das Hummelbuch*," Frau Hoffmann told me proudly. "It's a children's text," she said, flipping back the pages and then pointing, "you can see right here that it was published in 1934. My copy is one of only five thousand that were

Below, from left: HUM 340, Letter to Santa Claus; HUM 396, Ride Into Christmas; HUM 301, Christmas Angel; HUM 194, Watchful Angel; HUM 343, Christmas Song.

printed in the first edition. Sister Maria Innocentia's illustrations are accompanied by verses and text from the Viennese folk writer Margarete Seemann." Taking a closer look at the cover, I noticed a drawing of a rather large, distinctive, bee and the book's title written in a difficult-to-decipher, flourishy German script.

"That is a *Hummel*, a bumblebee," Frau Hoffmann explained. "Berta's mother had given her

the nickname *'das Hummele,'* which means 'little bumblebee'. Later, the bumblebee became Berta's personal trademark on many of her artworks." Carefully turning the pages again, I came across several cards that had been tucked inside the book. They were some of the original art cards featuring color reproductions of Sister Maria Innocentia's paintings. "Ah, yes," Frau Hoffmann nodded, when I held one up to her. "I collected these beautiful cards long ago."

In Germany, the Christmas celebration extends to December 26. Opposite page: HUM 261, Angel Duet.

Later, I helped Frau Hoffmann in the kitchen, preparing the traditional Christmas meal of roast goose stuffed with apples, homemade red cabbage, and soft, white *Kartoffelknödel*, which are also known as *Klöss* or *Reiberknödel*—the yummy and very filling potato dumplings which my father always referred to as "grandma's cannonballs." They did have a funny way of sinking to the bottom of the pot, I thought, as I dropped them, one by one, into the salted, boiling water. After about twenty minutes, they were bobbing around on top again, letting us know they were cooked and ready to be eaten.

When celebrating Christmas in Germany, there is the added bonus of waking up on the twenty-sixth of December, turning on a radio and still hearing the familiar

holiday carols that had been played throughout Advent. The *"zweiter Weihnachtsfeiertag"*—second Christmas holiday—is traditionally the day when families gather together with friends and distant relatives.

"Stille Nacht, Heilige Nacht! Alles schläft, einsam wacht. Nur das traute hochheilige Paar, holder Knabe im lockigen Haar, schlaf in himmlischer Ruh, schlaf in himmlischer Ruh!"... I thought of the German lyrics to "Silent Night" as I sat in the Hoffmanns' cozy warm *Stube*, enjoying the radiance of the flickering wax candles on the Christmas tree and the Advent wreath. I looked out the window into the dark and peaceful winter landscape, reflecting on what I had experienced these past few days and the added meaning this song now had for me.

The Chimney Sweep

ANYTIME YOU SPOT A KAMINKEHRER," my grandmother used to tell me, "it is considered an omen of good luck, especially in the days around New Year's," so I felt particularly fortunate the day I saw not one, but two, chimney sweeps walking down the street! Dressed in black from head to toe, they were wearing their traditional work clothes, topped off with tall, top hats, which are worn only at special times of the year. "When the *Kaminkehrer* came to our house to clean the chimney, it was indeed a special day," I could hear my grandmother saying. "My mother always left three fresh eggs in that lovely hat of his, which he would leave upturned on a table while he was up on the roof working." The increased use of modern oil and gas heating means the

> The infrequent sighting of a Bavarian chimney sweep in traditional work clothes is considered a definite omen of good luck.

Kaminkehrer comes only about two times a year, rather than calling monthly as in years gone by, so on this special day I wasn't the only one who stopped for this very rare encounter with traditional good fortune. Some young children stopped to look too, gazing at the chimney sweeps with wide eyes and running over to greet them and touch their magic-looking jackets. I soon found myself extending my right hand to shake theirs as they passed by, thinking my grandmother would have done the same, and I was pleased to see afterwards that some black soot—some "lucky" black soot, I hoped—had rubbed off on my hand.

In addition to the chimney sweep, other "Glücksbringer" (lucky charms) include four-leaf clovers, horseshoes and pigs. HUM 12, Chimney Sweep.

New Year's Eve and Epiphany

D IE NEUJAHRSNACHT STILL UND KLAR, *dentet auf ein gutes Jahr."* There is a popular belief that on New Year's Eve, or *Silvester,* as it is called, if the night is clear and filled with twinkling stars, it is a sure sign the coming year will be a good one. But between the wishes of *"Guten Rutsch!"* and *"Prosit Neujahr!"* the good-natured and superstitious Bavarians are not ones to leave anything to chance. They prefer to give their New Year's luck an added boost at midnight by making as much noise and racket as possible, with exploding firecrackers and colorful fireworks, to scare away all of the ghosts and bad luck of the old year. And if there are still some unlucky spirits loafing about on New Year's Day, the traditional loud bangs of the *Neujahrsschiessen,* which involves shooting off several rounds of high-caliber muskets, are intended to frighten away any unwanted stragglers. The town of Pottenstein, in the *Fränkische Schweiz,* marks Epiphany, on January 6, with a traditional festival of lights and bonfires which burn throughout the night and cast a warm glow on the town. Their tradition is rooted in man's fear of the darkness and cold, and the witches and evil spirits that lurked around in it.

Throughout the countryside, between New Year's and the Epiphany, children bearing good wishes go from house to house with an important mission. I happened to spot three of them, costumed as the biblical Three Wise Men of the East, scribbling something above the Hoffmanns' front door with a piece of white chalk. After singing a traditional Bavarian song, they told me their names were Caspar, Melchior and Balthasar. Looking up at their handwork, I read "C + M + B" followed by the year, and asked, "what does this mean?"

"They are our initials," one answered, and a second one

The annual festival of lights on Epiphany in the romantic town of Pottenstein has been held in its present form since the nineteenth century.

added, "but the letters also stand for *'Christus Mansionem Benedicat,'* a Latin phrase asking God to bless this house." "It is a wish of good luck," the third one chimed in. I learned later, when telling Herr Hoffmann what I had seen, that the centuries'-old tradition is based, in part, on a medieval legend that the Three Wise Men's bones are housed in a golden shrine at the cathedral in Cologne.

Crafting Hummel
Figurines

The creation of a Hummel figurine begins when a master sculptor makes a three-dimensional clay model from one of Sister Maria Innocentia's images.

MY SEEMINGLY INSATIABLE CRUSADE to experience as much of Bavaria and its rich traditions as possible, and my growing fascination with Sister Maria Innocentia Hummel brought me, on a cold and gray day in late January, to northeast Bavaria and the famed Goebel porcelain factory, which was founded in 1871. It was a personal pilgrimage, of sorts; now that I had looked at some of Sister Maria Innocentia's drawings and cards, I wanted to see for myself how their essence is transformed into the bright and lively three-dimensional porcelain figurines that had first caught my attention so many years ago.

W. Goebel Porzellanfabrik is called a factory, but I quickly saw that it is not one in the traditional sense of the word. As I looked around, it immediately became clear to me that the work here is done not by machines, but rather by hundreds of pairs of careful hands.

The first set of skilled hands belongs to a master sculptor, who makes a three-dimensional clay model based on an image by Sister Maria Innocentia. Once the sculpture is complete, it is carefully cut into workable sections that become the basis for a series of molds. Each piece of the model has its own mold; sometimes there are as many as forty separate pieces for a figurine, my guide explained to me.

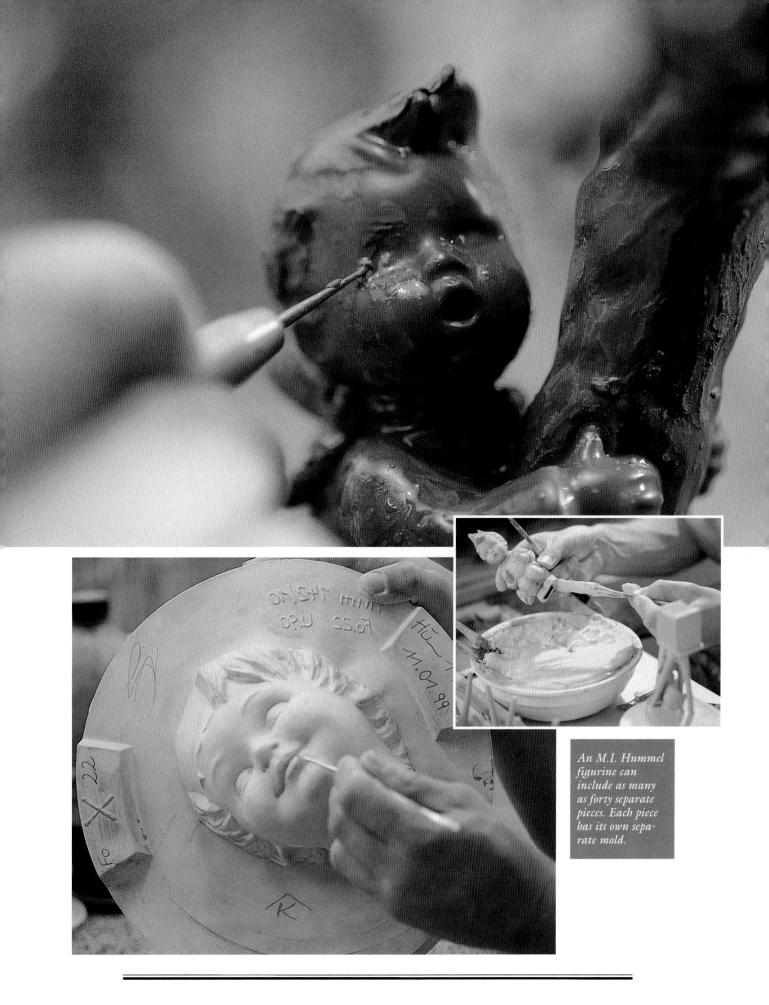

An M.I. Hummel figurine can include as many as forty separate pieces. Each piece has its own separate mold.

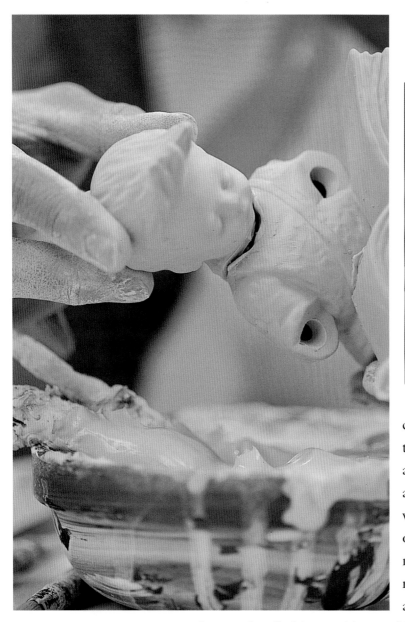

"Even a relatively small figurine can have as many as twelve distinct parts," she added. Looking at the pieces on the table, I was amazed to see that the tiniest wisp of hair, a small hat feather, or even the delicate handle of a miniature basket requires a separate mold. Passing through another room filled with count-

Using liquid slip as glue, above, a figurine is assembled from its parts. After a first firing, figurines are dipped in a glazing bath, right.

less stacks of white working molds, my escort explained that these molds can be used only a limited number of times before losing their detail, so there is a continual need at the factory to make identical, new molds for each figurine design, and there are many sets of hands at work in this area.

When the molds have been created and the pieces of the figurine poured and cast separately, there is the delicate task of assembling each figurine, while still wet, from its assorted parts. Once an assembler has neatly joined together the figurine's many parts, using a liquid slip as glue, the figurine has its first kiln firing. Each figurine is then

hand-dipped into a glazing bath that is tinted to ensure that the entire figurine is covered. After a second (glaze) firing, the figurine emerges, now shiny white.

Most memorable, for me, was my visit to the painting department, where a figurine is first given its individual expression, those unmistakable eyes and mouth providing a striking contrast to the shiny white porcelain. The flesh tones come next, followed by those round rosy cheeks. I peered over the shoulders of several painters as they added ever more details: stripes on jackets, suspenders, tiny flowers, socks, even the soles of the shoes. Each time a color was added, a bit of it was taken off to achieve the desired effect.

The painstaking attention to detail, the high quality of workmanship and the discernible pride in their handicraft tradition—traits I had observed during visits to other Bavarian artisans and craftsmen—were all evident at every stage of Goebel's production process.

Altogether, hundreds of individual hand operations are involved in the

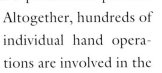

Hundreds of individual hand operations are involved in the completion of just one M.I. Hummel figurine.

completion of one M.I. Hummel figurine. As I beheld the countless figurines standing in tidy rows around me, Goebel's mission to bring the artwork of Sister Maria Innocentia to three-dimensional life seemed staggering. Before parting, my guide left me with these words: "Here at Goebel," she said, "we have a saying that 'Hands make Goebel.'" I told her that after what I had seen, it was clear to me that there was a lot of heart involved, too.

Fasching

THEY ARE CALLED "DIE NÄRRISCHEN TAGE," and they are the days in the dead of winter when it is still cold, dark, damp and dreary, and when it seems as though all of Bavaria has gone a bit mad. The atmosphere is created by parades of wildly colorful and imaginative costumes—frightening furry creatures, witches, men dressed as women—as well as by a wide assortment of regionally mysterious wooden masks. *Fasching* is the name for this pre-Lenten craziness, which originated in pagan times, when men felt helpless against the wrath of nature. The pagan response was to make a

"Die närrischen Tage" (the foolish days) of Fasching *take place each year between Epiphany and Ash Wednesday.*

The collection of wooden masks–"G'sichtln"– above is from Werdenfelser Land. Each one is worn at a specific time during Fasching.

ruckus, blowing horns, ringing bells, screaming and yodeling, and donning ghastly masks to scare away the unwelcome demons of winter.

Each wooden mask, with its unique and clever design, has a specific meaning and is worn, according to tradition, at a specific time during *Fasching*. Some have been in the same family for generations. My grandmother had one tucked away in a trunk that she would pull out now and then, telling me it had been in her mother's family for more than a hundred years and was last worn by one of her uncles. "The important thing was not wearing the mask," she would explain, shaking her head, "no, anyone could do that. You had to be able to 'play' the mask too."

91

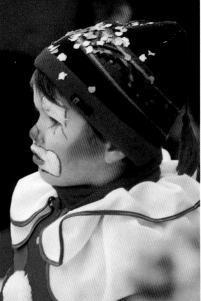

The Fasching *festivities* come to a head on Faschingsdienstag *(known in the United States as Fat Tuesday)*, when the child at left joined in the fun. *Opposite page, from left:* HUM 616, Parade of Lights; HUM 328, Carnival.

At Fasching, *children enjoy dressing like clowns, painting their faces and sometimes wearing silly wigs. The pre-Lenten craziness is basically about foolish fun.*

SPRING

The Barrel Maker

T HEY ARE CALLED, IN BAVARIAN, SCHÄFFLER, but I knew them as coopers, or barrel makers, practicing an age-old profession, which, like so many others, is disappearing. So it was with much excitement that I happened upon the workshop of one who still takes great joy in making a barrel out of wood. This is a skilled trade that demands nothing short of absolute precision: a leaky barrel, or keg, after all, doesn't do much for business!

"Some Bavarian breweries still use wooden kegs to store their beer," this *Schäffler* told me, "but not as many as used to. Some of our work involves making repairs to used barrels, like those damaged ones over there on the floor. Lucky for us, distilleries, which make brandy, bourbon, whiskey and scotch, have still found no replacement for a sturdy, fragrant wooden barrel." After pausing briefly to hammer the steel band down tighter

around the arched wooden staves of the
barrel he was making, he continued,
"Centuries ago, the *Schäffler* were important, well-respected and necessary craftsmen in Bavaria. In Munich, after the plague
in the early sixteenth century, it was the
Schäffler who, largely unaffected by the epi-
demic, finally convinced the people it was
okay to go back out onto the
streets again. They did this by

*The Coopers' Dance,
below, is performed
every seven years to
commemorate the
people's deliverance
from the plague of
1517.*

performing a special dance, which the people came out to watch, and
special *Schäffler* groups do this every seven years since then. This
dance is memorialized on Munich's *Glockenspiel* carillon, where figures of the costumed coopers dance every day."

Munich

I WAS ABLE TO SEE FOR MYSELF THE DANCE of the coopers on Munich's *Glockenspiel*, and remember the barrel maker's story, when I visited the Bavarian capital soon after. I was struck by the stark contrast between this vibrant, lively and very cosmopolitan city and the peacefulness of the surrounding countryside where I had been staying. It was a thrill to look upon the history and beauty of Munich's storied settings, still standing, as they had for centuries, a quiet reminder of how far I was from home. Had this city generated similar feelings of awe and admiration in Berta Hummel? She was younger than I, barely eighteen, when she moved to the capital in 1927 to study at the Academy of Applied Arts. I couldn't help but wonder at her reaction.

The neo-Gothic Neues Rathaus (New Town Hall), below, is on Munich's Marienplatz. In the Glockenspiel, left appears a scene of the Coopers' Dance.

A gilded figure of
the Virgin Mary as
Patron Saint of
Bavaria, above, is
framed by the towers
of the landmark
Frauenkirche
Cathedral.

Trachten

Nowhere is Bavaria's love of folk culture, tradition and regional identity more apparent than in the wearing of *Trachten* (*G'wand* in Bavarian), the popular and well-recognized folk attire, which seems to have as many individualized variations as there are individuals outfitted in it. The rich boiled wools, the smooth, satiny silks and the buttery soft leathers are complemented by intricate embroidery, buttons of shiny silver or *Hirschhorn* (deer antler), decorative chains, patterned lace, exquisite hat feathers, and, even, the ornamental hats themselves. These colorful garments, though, are more than mere flights of fancy; from head-to-toe, to the tiniest detail, these costumes are a sum of their parts, the total of which conveys a specific story about the individual wearing the clothes. Is he rich, a hunter or a farmer; is she single, from *Oberfranken* or maybe *Oberbayern*? Without a single word being spoken, it's possible to know the answer. A costume with lots of silver buttons, coins and chains, for example, was an indication of one's excellent financial standing, while, in some areas, the color of a woman's crown-like *Riegelhaube*, worn at the back of the head, told you if she was single (silver), married (gold) or widowed (black or dark blue).

Whether restored, handmade or purchased, these exquisitely accessorized and detailed outfits are by no means inexpensive, so today the most elaborate versions are usually worn only by members of local *Trachtenvereinen*—clubs, which are dedicated to the preservation of Bavaria's folk history and culture. For them, the garments represent an undeniable link with the region's rich and colorful past.

Lederhosen are perhaps the most recognizable of all the various forms of *Trachten*, so it was with much interest and curiosity that I went to a *Lederhosenmacher*, where the unique leather trousers are still carefully made and embroidered by hand. "Where do you come from," the inquisitive tailor asked, before I could utter a single word upon entering his shop, "Munich, Regensburg, or perhaps even Schwangau?"

"Far from it," I laughed in response, "why do you ask?" He told me that the answer to his question provides a clue as to what type of *Lederhosen* a person might be looking for, because traditional styles vary region by region. So, it was with much amusement, I finally told him, "I'm from America," adding,

"do you make anything special for over there?" "Ah, yes," he said, "there are many Americans who have bought my *Lederhosen*." With that, he brought out several pairs and I ended up spending an hour or so trying on *Lederhosen* in a variety of lengths and colors from light green to black, while he continued chatting.

The color of a man's Lederhosen, *as well as the patterns and color of the embroidery, give clues about where he is from.*

"Historically," he said, "*Kurze*, short *Lederhosen*, in a brownish, natural shade, were, and still are, the work clothes of hunters and foresters who live in the *Gebirge*, alpine areas like Oberstdorf in the Allgäu, Mittenwald in Werdenfelser Land and Bischhofswiesen in Berchtesgadener Land. The most noticeable differ-

ence between a pair from each place is the color of the silk thread used in the embroidery." I admired the beautiful stitchery of intertwined oak leaves and flowers, as I gently stroked the soft texture of the buckskin leather. The tailor told me it can take twenty-one hours to make a pair of *Kurze*, and twenty-seven hours to make a pair of *Bundhosen*, a knicker-like design which laces at the knee. When I had finally decided which pair I wanted to buy, he nodded approvingly, saying, "A '*richtiger Bayer*'—real Bavarian—wears only black *Lederhosen*."

Bavaria's endearing folk costumes, known as Trachten, *come in a wide array of regionally distinctive variations.*

The wearing of Trachten *represents an undeniable link with Bavaria's rich and colorful past. Opposite page:* HUM 437, Tuba Player.

No detail is overlooked by Trachten *clubs, which are dedicated to preserving regional folk culture and history.*
Below, right: HUM 240, Little Drummer.

A special festival called the Gautrachtenfest offers a unique opportunity to see numerous types of Trachten in every combination and color imaginable.

Bamberg

WITH MY STAY IN BAVARIA AT ABOUT the halfway point, I found myself in Bamberg, sitting at a long wooden table, in a popular old beer hall, and drinking a *Rauchbier*, a rather distinctive smoky tasting beer made from smoked malt. To me it looked as dark as the paneling that covered the walls. I reflected upon the past few days in this dream-like region where, indeed, one of my lifetime dreams had finally come true.

Bamberg is one of the many gems of *Franken*. The city's narrow, cobblestone streets and curving alleyways combine with the impressive spires and the clean, decorative lines of the city's *Fachwerk* (half-timbered) houses and other varied architectural styles to create a different por-

Bamberg's "Little Venice," above, is a well-known area of fishermen's and boatmen's houses. Opposite page: A rustic Fachwerk *house is covered with vines.*

trait of Bavaria. I was particularly fascinated by the historic Old Town Hall, which stands in the middle of a river!

Bamberg is not far from the small village where my grandmother had spent her youth—a place where, just a couple days earlier, my lifetime of curiosity had finally been satisfied. There I was, standing outside a very old farmhouse, taking in each and every detail. Although it was the first time I had been there, everything looked

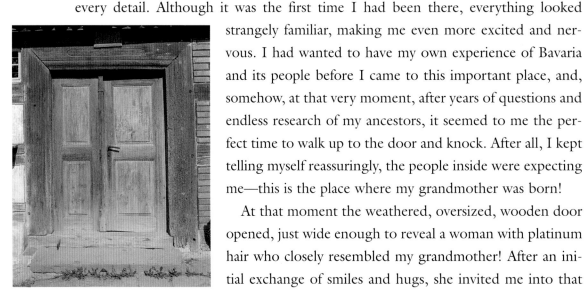

A variety of architectural styles, from Romanesque to Baroque, typify the picturesque city of Bamberg.

strangely familiar, making me even more excited and nervous. I had wanted to have my own experience of Bavaria and its people before I came to this important place, and, somehow, at that very moment, after years of questions and endless research of my ancestors, it seemed to me the perfect time to walk up to the door and knock. After all, I kept telling myself reassuringly, the people inside were expecting me—this is the place where my grandmother was born!

At that moment the weathered, oversized, wooden door opened, just wide enough to reveal a woman with platinum hair who closely resembled my grandmother! After an initial exchange of smiles and hugs, she invited me into that

wonderful house where she introduced me to the rest of *my* relatives. We spent much of that memorable day, and a good part of the next one, exchanging family lore, looking through old photo albums and sharing some long-overdue laughs.

Contemplating it all, in this popular if noisy Bamberg establishment, it was as though the past couple of days were but a sweet dream. But as I held the aged black-and-white photo that my newly found relatives gave me before departing, I looked into the eyes of the child who was my grandmother, and felt that, finally, all of my childhood questions had been answered.

Sister Maria Innocentia's Tale Unfolds

S EVERAL WEEKS LATER, BOARDING YET another train, I spotted someone I had met before, not long after I had arrived in Germany. Yes, I thought excitedly, I am not one to forget a face, especially not hers; it was the mysterious woman who had told me so much about Berta Hummel! *"Grüss Gott,"* I greeted her, *"ist der Platz noch frei?"* asking whether she minded if I sat in the empty seat beside her. She looked at me with her animated eyes and nodded graciously, *"Ja, bitte,"* adding with a smile, "you look familiar, have we met before?"

In Bavaria, everyday life includes a mixture of plain and storybook settings. Opposite page: HUM 350, On Holiday.

"We were on a train together last autumn and you told me some interesting stories about Berta Hummel," I explained, telling her I was traveling around Bavaria to learn more about my German ancestors and their colorful traditions.

"Oh, yes," she remembered with a smile, and then, without my saying another word, she continued where she had left off months before. "Berta's grandfather, Jakob Hummel, did a lot of traveling too. He was originally from the town of Eningen in Württemberg and was part of a family of traveling salesmen. They would wander through the countryside, carrying their wares and notions on a wooden *Krax'n*, which they wore on their backs, often stopping at fairs, here and there, to make some sales. That was how Jakob eventually ended up in Massing, founding his business direct on the market square in 1874." She paused for a moment, as if deep in thought, and then, leaning toward me, said in her Bavarian dialect, carefully articulated so that I could more easily

understand, "Not many people know this, but Berta's father, Adolf, had aspired to be a *Bildhauer* or a *Holzschnitzer*—a sculptor or a woodcarver. It was his father, Jakob, though, who encouraged him to enter the family business and become a merchant. Berta's mother, Victoria, meanwhile, came from a conservative, farming family, much like my own."

As I digested her words, I thought that this woman, with her friendly smile and gentle laugh, reminded me a bit of my grandmother. I wondered why I hadn't noticed this the last time we met. Finally I said, "The Hummels must have both taken great pride in the talent and achievements of their daughter." We sat a while longer, talking and laughing, as an eclectic mix of plain and storybook settings passed by the window of the train. It seemed as though only a short time had passed, when in fact it had been over an hour, so I was both surprised, and disappointed, when the train began slowing to a stop at my point of departure.

"Herzlichen Dank," I thanked the woman, as I quickly gathered together my belongings. "Make sure you visit the Siessen convent while you are in Bavaria," she said, taking my right hand in both of hers, patting it gently. "It is where Berta spent her life as a sister and did many of her portraits of children."

"I will," I promised her, "I will." I hurried towards the door. As the train started to slowly pull away from the station, a window suddenly opened, and she called out to me, "When you get there, be sure to ask for Sister Lena."

"Sister Lena?" I shouted back, a bit confused.

"Yes," she said, waving, a big smile still on her face, "Sister Lena is my sister!"

As the train rushed off into the distance, I stood beside the tracks, waving to my new friend and whispering her a heartfelt, *"Pfüagod."*

Easter

EASTER IS AN EAGERLY AWAITED HOLIDAY in Bavaria, not only for its colorful and solemn traditions but because, against the backdrop of reawakening blooms and foliage, it offers hope of a welcome respite for the winter-weary. There are the traditional outdoor Easter markets, where treasure-seekers can find exquisitely decorated and hand-painted eggs, the dignified religious processions and, in parts of *Franken*, especially towns and villages in the *Fränkische Schweiz*, there is the intriguing custom of decorating local water wells and fountains with elaborate displays of festive garlands, colorful ribbons and hundreds of vibrantly painted eggs. These cheery creations, called *Osterbrunnen*, are a celebration of water's role as a symbol for the existence of life.

A Karfreitag (Good Friday) procession, above, stops for a moment of prayer. Opposite page: Osterbrunnen are an Easter tradition. Left: HUM 55, Saint George.

The Easter weekend also marks the start, in some parts of Bavaria, of the traditional *Georgiritt* observances, magnificent spectacles of strong horses and handsomely outfitted riders in honor of Saint George, the legendary dragon-slayer who, like the revered Saint Leonhard, is a patron saint of horses. Saint George's feast day falls on April 23, and parades in honor of this much-loved saint take place in towns like Aidenbach in *Niederbayern* and Hausen and Aigen am Inn in the *Oberpfalz*. A *Georgiritt* that is especially well-known takes place on *Ostermontag*, the day after Easter, in Traunstein by the Chiemsee lake in *Oberbayern*.

Maypoles

H EY, LOOK OVER HERE!" IT SEEMED to call out, sleekly clad in an intricate pattern of white-and-blue and reaching high into the clear, blue Bavarian sky. As I looked up to admire its decorative features, I thought that in Bavaria it's difficult not to notice maypoles. You can find them throughout the countryside, in the center of nearly every small town and village, and not only in May, as custom originally dictated, but throughout the entire year! The practice of raising a modern-day maypole involves so much work and expense that these very visible works of civic art and pride are left standing for

four or five years, after which they are finally taken down and replaced with new ones. The custom of raising a new maypole is called the *Maibaumaufstellen* and it only happens on one day a year—May 1st.

Maypoles are a common sight in the quaint Bavarian countryside. Left, a traditional Maibaumaufstellen takes place on the first of May.

Some places still follow the age-old tradition of raising these immense icons of spring toward their upright positions by hand. This strenuous technique requires a certain degree of patience and the use of special wooden poles, bound together on one end with thick rope to support the tremendous weight of the maypole as it is being lifted. Also, and perhaps most importantly, it requires the strength of dozens of mighty Bavarian men! *"Schiabts O!"*—*"Push!"*—someone shouts and gradually, inch-by-inch, the maypole is raised to its place of honor.

No *Maibaumaufstellen* is complete, of course, without liter-sized mugs of cold beer, traditional music, singing and folk dances, like the *Bandltanz*. "We would stand around a smaller maypole, dressed

No two maypoles are exactly alike. Each is decorated with wreaths, flags and special wooden shields that tell a story about the area.

Opposite page: *"Faithful to the good old tradition"* reads a wooden plaque on this maypole. *Above:* HUM 348, Ring Around the Rosie.

in our finest Sunday clothes," my grandmother would recall, "each of us holding the end of a white or blue ribbon. When the music started playing, we danced in a circle around the pole, and, if there were no missteps, halfway through the *Bandltanz*, we could see that our ribbons had created a replica of the Bavarian flag's well-known white-blue diamond pattern."

No two maypoles are exactly alike. Each is individually groomed with a particular combination of flags or ribbons, wreaths, garlands and painted wooden shields to tell a story about the immediate area and what the people there are known for—whether it's local folk customs or folk costumes, sport clubs, farming or beer brewing. An age-old superstition, still popularly accepted, holds that everyone and everything within sight of a maypole are protected against bad luck, evil and disasters, such as flood and fire. This superstition explains the maypole's most conspicuous, and prominent, central location.

The Wagon-Wheel Maker

ONE SPRING MORNING I HAPPENED UPON one of the Hoffmann's sons in the barn where he was busy assembling something. It appeared to be a wagon wheel, and it was—a replacement for the old wagon they use in the fields. As I watched him at work, I was amazed at the amount of skill and precision required for this largely fogotten craft which, for centuries, was a vital trade in any town or village—but that was in the days before the automobile.

"My great-grandfather was a *Wagner*, or carriage maker, and so was his father before him," he said proudly, adding, "It was a trade often passed from father to son, but for me it is just a hobby, a connection with the past, I guess you could call it. Some of these tools here have been in our family for generations." I watched a while longer, marveling that this wheel, something which would eventually bear so much weight, could be made of wood—and without the use of a single nail, bolt or glue.

The trade of the Wagner *was often passed from father to son. A* Brotzeit, *midmorning snack, below, awaits the* Wagner. *Opposite page:* HUM 226, The Mail is Here.

120

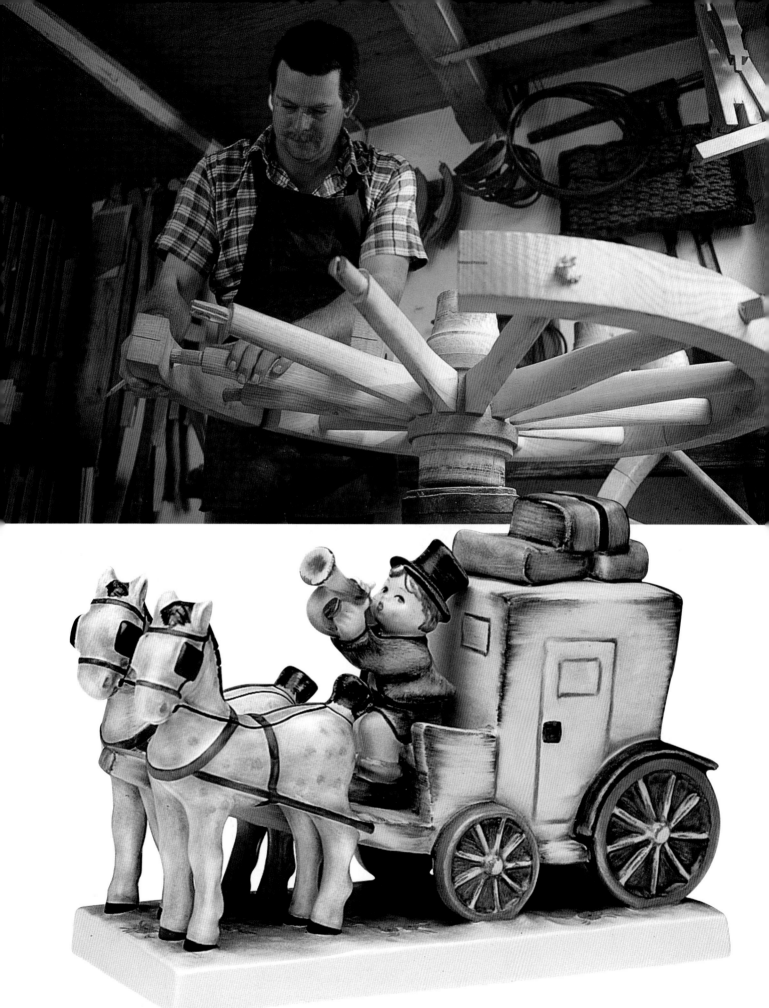

121

Pilgrimages

T HEY ARRIVE BY FOOT, BY TRAIN, OR by bus. For some, it is a journey of hours, and for others it takes days. Tens of thousands of pilgrims, every year, from May through November, make their way to various religious shrines in Bavaria believed to hold miraculous, healing powers and answers to prayers of faith. These *Wallfahrten*—or pilgrimages—have a long history, some dating back to the Middle Ages, and others to the seventeenth century and the state's former Wittelsbach rulers. There are more than four hundred pilgrimage sites alone devoted to the worship of the Blessed Virgin Mary who, in Bavaria, also holds the honorary title of *"Patrona Bavariae,"* the patron, or protector, of the land. Still others are dedicated to Christ and various saints. Chief among these pilgrimage destinations is the Chapel of Grace in Altötting, a town

Opposite page: Pilgrimages and religious processions, like this one in Fränkische Schweiz on Corpus Christi, have a long tradition.

A Martel, *wayside shrine,* as at left, is a common sight in rural Bavaria. *Below, from left:* HUM 84, Worship; HUM 28, Wayside Devotion; HUM 23, Adoration; HUM 183, Forest Shrine.

√ mine
from Arabelle

commonly referred to as the heart of Catholic Bavaria, and which, singularly, symbolizes the deep-seated devotion and beliefs of the Bavarian people. Other important sites include: Maria Eich, Inchenhofen, Andechs, Birkenstein, Scheyern, Würzburg, Wies near Steingaden, Mariabuchen, Maria Birnbaum, the Mariahilfberg in Amberg, and Vierzehnheiligen near Lichtenfels.

One of the oldest and most distinct pilgrimages in Bavaria is the ceremonial *Kötztinger Pfingstritt*, which coincides with the Catholic church's observance of Pentecost. More than nine hundred men, handsomely dressed in long, dark blue jackets, black pants and wide-brimmed, black hats—folk costumes typical of the *Oberpfalz* region—ride atop their decorated horses in a procession of prayer from the town of Kötzting, in the Bavarian Forest, to the pilgrimage church of St. Nikolas, in Steinbühl. The tradition of this nine-mile round-trip journey dates back to the year 1412, when a priest, thankful he had made the trip safely under cover of darkness, vowed to do it every year.

Of all the religious-oriented holidays in Bavaria, *Fronleichnam*, or *Corpus Christi*, which commemorates the institution and gift of the Eucharist and is celebrated by the Catholic church on the second Thursday after Pentecost, is considered the most important. Religious banners, candles and statues are carried in reverent, colorful processions, some of which, like those in Augsburg, Freising, Munich and Würzburg, date back to the Middle Ages. A procession of particular note is the one that takes place near the town of Murnau on the Staffelsee lake.

SUMMER

In a Bavarian Beer Garden

"HOPFEN UND MALZ, GOTT ERHALT'S." "Hops and malt, God save them." How often I had spotted this German expression during these past months I cannot exactly say, but it wasn't until recently that I fully understood the true meaning behind the words, as I sat in the cool shade of a giant chestnut tree and witnessed an annual summer migration when, it seems, all of Bavaria flocks to the outdoors in search of a vacant seat in the casual and relaxed atmosphere of a beer garden. This one pastime, I quickly observed, is probably closest to the Bavarian heart, and it embodies an essential element of local custom and culture, while paying homage to Bavaria's favorite liquid refreshment—*Bier!* Hops and barley malt are two of only four ingredients allowed to be used in the brewing of German beer. The other two are yeast and water. This so-called *Reinheitsgebot* is one of the world's oldest food purity laws, having been first decreed in the early sixteenth century and, not surprisingly, by a Bavarian. I still find it amazing that these simple ingredients are responsible for creating such a wide variety of thirst quenchers, from the amber *Helles* lager and the slightly bitter *Pils* (Pilsner), to the *Bock*, a light- or dark-colored strong beer, the dark *Dunkles*, Oktoberfest's *Marzen*, also known as *Festbier*, and the highly carbonated *Weizen* or *Weissbier*, a particular Bavarian favorite often served

Beer gardens and folk fests, above, are popular gathering places in the summer. Bavarian hops, left, are one of the primary ingredients of beer. Opposite page: HUM 87, For Father.

Fragrant, perennial spiraling vines of hops are a common sight in the Hallertau, the world's largest hops-growing region.

with a slice of lemon.

Bavaria can boast more than half the total breweries to be found in all of Germany—about seven hundred in all—and in the summer it seems as though each of them has at least one beer garden, usually many more. One day, as I sat in one of these welcome oases from the burdens and stress of everyday life, someone told me that in the Munich area alone there are enough beer garden seats to accommodate more than 100,000 people! Where better, I thought, to wile away those hot afternoons and warm evenings than in the company of colleagues, friends or family, at a place where the beer is cold and the typical picnic-like fare can range from giant, fresh-baked *Brezen* (pretzels) and spreadable *Obatzder* cheese to spiral-sliced and salted white radishes, grilled sausages, sauerkraut, delicious roast chicken or *Schweinshax'n* (roast leg of pork), grilled spare ribs and *Steckerlfisch* (fish, like mackerel or trout, grilled whole on a stick).

"Hopfen und Malz, Gott erhalt's." The same words crossed my mind again as I traveled one weekend by bicycle through the heart of *Altbayern*, or old Bavaria, passing splendid settings of rolling hills and meadows, quaint villages and row after row of Bavaria's most sought-after crop. *"Grünes Gold"* (green gold) is what they call it here, or more simply, hops. Tucked between the Danube and Isar rivers, the

Hallertau, or *Holledau,* as it is known locally, is the largest hops-growing region in the world, and in late summer these fragrant, perennial spiraling vines are reaching high into the blue Bavarian skies and their pre-harvest homestretch. Each vine has the potential to yield enough hops for a staggering three hundred one-liter Bavarian mugs of beer!

There is an old saying in the *Hallertau,* which goes: *"Der Hopfen will jeden Tag seinen Herrn sehen."*—"The hops want to see their master every day." I was told the expression refers to the large amount of work, time and money a farmer must invest in a hops crop before it finally finds its way into various beers around the world. As I thought back on all those Bavarian beer gardens, however, it occurred to me that the special attention given to the herby hops didn't end in these fields.

Embroidered Masterpieces

A T FIRST GLANCE, IN THE MORNING LIGHT, they looked like canvas masterpieces—stunning works in progress coming to life with beautiful, carefully
applied brushstrokes in an array of appealing hues. It was only when I moved into the
room to take a closer look that I realized the objects of my admiration were being created not with paint on canvas, but with thread on fabric. "You
must be the Michelangelo and Van Gogh of embroidery," I said
to the all-too-modest Dominican sisters, as I delighted in a fine
and detailed rendering of the legendary Saint George slaying a
dragon; it was on the front of what eventually would be a new
flag.

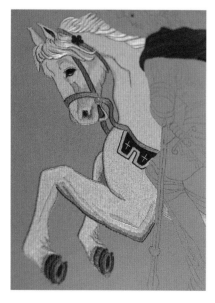

"Many of the *Fahnen* (flags) carried in Bavaria's innumerable
religious processions and folk events have had
their beginnings in a convent like ours," offered
one of the sisters, quickly adding, "it can take
months to finish just one." The sisters showed
me some of their magnificent handwork, which
included not only flags and banners, but reli-

*Many of the
embroidered flags
carried at tradi-
tional folk events
and processions
had their begin-
nings in a convent.*

134

gious vestments and even a vertical pattern of alpine flowers that would one day decorate the suspenders attached to someone's *Lederhosen*! The minute and painstaking detail of the exquisite treasures I beheld was simply breathtaking, and I could truly appreciate the amount of time, love and care that went into each and every stitch.

The painstaking creations of these Dominican sisters, above, can take months to complete. Below: HUM 255, A Stitch in Time.

"My grandmother enjoyed embroidery," I told them. "She always tried to get me interested in it but, unfortunately, I never had enough patience for it, much less for a project as considerable as these."

It wasn't long after my visit to the convent that I happened upon an even wider selection of these stately flags at a special festival called a *Gautrachtenfest*. The event, complete with a giant beer tent and attended by dozens of *Trachten* clubs from near and far, afforded me a unique opportunity to see not only flags, but also numerous types of folk costumes in every combination and color imaginable. The beautiful flags and costumes took on an added richness for me as I remembered the sisters, patiently embroidering in that sun-filled room in the convent.

Rothenburg ob der Tauber

ONE OF MY FONDEST WISHES WHILE I was in Bavaria was to see the medieval walled towns of Rothenburg ob der Tauber and Dinkelsbühl, to wander through the old townscapes, cobblestones underfoot, and along the ancient fortifications, surrounded by the architecture and ambience of a forgotten time. Today both towns are pilgrimage sites, of sorts, attracting tens of thousands of tourists each year. With a bit of imagination, however, it is possible to transport yourself back in time.

My grandmother often told me a wonderful story about Rothenburg, one of the few towns in Bavaria still preserved in its original form. The legendary *Meistertrunk* is an event that is commemorated not only yearly with a special festival, but also daily on

the clock above the town's *Ratstrinkstube* (city hall drinking cellar). Finally in Rothenburg, I recalled my grandmother's tale.

"In the year 1631, during a religious struggle called the Thirty Years' War, the commander of the Catholic forces entered the Protestant imperial city of Rothenburg ob der Tauber, where he was abjectly offered a giant tankard filled with more than three liters—almost one gallon—of wine. Struck with a rather mischievous idea, he said he'd spare the town if anyone could empty the tankard in one try. It seemed an impossible task, but the mayor volunteered anyway, and succeeded, sparing the town." As

Rothenburg ob der Tauber, a popular Bavarian destination in Franken, is still preserved in its original walled, medieval form.

I continued to take in the timeless beauty around me, I felt that I, too, owed the mayor a debt of thanks, for his selfless determination, and his magnanimous thirst!

Rothenburg is only one of many places in Bavaria that reenact key moments from their past.

The summer months, in fact, are filled with an interesting array of historical and religious-oriented festivals, in addition to countless *Trachten*, wine and folk fests. Certainly the most famous is Oberammergau's world-renowned Passion Play, held every ten years in

The all-day performances of Oberammergau's famous Passion Play, above, are staged by local villagers.
Right: HUM 369, Follow the Leader.

keeping with a promise made by the town in 1633 as it was in the grip of the black plague. The *Drachenstich* is held annually in Furth im Wald, meanwhile, and memorializes the legend of Saint George and the ferocious dragon, and the

Kinderzeche Festwoche is an annual children's festival in Dinkelsbühl that also has its roots in the Thirty Years' War. But this is just a small sampling.

I was fortunate to see the *Landshuter Hochzeit 1475*, a historical pageant held every four years to reenact the colorful medieval nuptials of the daughter of a Polish king to the son of the duke of Landshut, which in 1475 was the capital of Bavaria. The jousting, juggling, music and fire-eating were topped only by the entertaining bridal procession through the old town and a visit to a typical camp from the Middle Ages. Someone told me that at the real wedding, under the duke's orders, Landshut's residents were includ-

ed in the marriage revelry, eating and drinking for a week for free! Lucky for Landshut, I thought, that not *every* detail is reenacted.

A quadrennial pageant in Landshut, right, reenacts the medieval nuptials of the son of Landshut's duke to a Polish king's daughter.

Lüftlmalerei

NOW THAT I HAD BEEN IN BAVARIA ALMOST a year, I had seen folk art in many unforgettable forms, from the delicate creations of the Bavarian Forest glass blowers to the amazingly detailed pewter miniatures of the Zinngiesser. When I traveled throughout *Oberbayern* I was especially fascinated by the ornamental masterpieces found painted on the facades of houses and buildings, a well-known type of folk art called *Lüftlmalerei*. These distinctive frescoes often depict scenes of fantasy, religion, folk culture, everyday life and protective patron saints. Created since the Middle Ages, these paintings, and the artists who painted them, indirectly got their German names from well-known *Lüftlmaler*, Oberammergau-born Franz Seraph Zwinck (1748-1792), who used the name of his family's house, *"Zum Lüftl,"* which means "breezy place," to advertise his trade.

Oberammergau-born Franz Seraph Zwinck is credited with giving the unique frescoed folk art of Lüftlmalerei *its distinctive name.*

Typical Lüftlmalerei motifs include protective patron saints, scenes of fantasy, religion, folk culture and everyday life.

Oberbayern is home to many splendid examples of Lüftlmalerei design, including Bavaria's beloved King Ludwig, left.

The Shepherd

SHEPHERDS CAN STILL BE FOUND IN Bavaria, as I happily observed one day when I met a *Schäfer*, tending a flock with his two trusted canine companions. The difficult, nomadic life of this age-old calling, though, is not as popular, or necessary, as it once was. So I took particular note of the special patch this shepherd wore proudly on his jacket, noting his achievement of seventy years in the profession.

Traditionally, a *Schäfer* cared for the sheep, and sometimes other animals as well, for an entire community and the community would,

> *Shepherds are still found in Bavaria. This one, below, has carefully tended his flocks for more than seventy years. Opposite page:* HUM 395, Shepherd Boy.

in turn, provide him with food and shelter. In some areas, like the *Fränkische Schweiz*, or Franconian Switzerland, the infertile, barren and hilly terrain was more suited to the tending of sheep than keeping cows or farming.

The Siessen Convent

MY YEAR-LONG VISIT TO BAVARIA was nearing an end, and I still had some unfinished business. So, one drizzly morning in late August, after passing through the town of Saulgau, I finally found myself approaching the Siessen convent, the former religious home of Sister Maria Innocentia Hummel. Surrounded by a placid sea of green fields, it seemed to rise up on the horizon before me.

The convent of the Franciscan sisters of Siessen is located in the state of Baden-Württemberg, north of Lake Constance, on Bavaria's southwestern border. A mother house and teaching convent, it is where the sisters receive instruction and training for their work in Franciscan-operated schools and missions in Germany and abroad. Berta Hummel arrived at Siessen on April 22, 1931, just a few short weeks after graduating from the Munich Academy of Applied

The Siessen convent, above, in the German state of Baden-Württemberg, is the former religious home of Sister Maria Innocentia.

The convent, I presumed, as I glanced at its exalted exteriors, had grown architecturally in the ensuing years between then and now, but it was my hope that the spirit of the women living inside had remained unchanged.

Sister Lena, who I had phoned a few weeks earlier, was expecting me. She smiled and warmly shook my hand when I arrived, introducing me to another of the sisters, Sister Dora, who, it appeared, was only a few years older than myself. "We know you have a great interest in Sister Maria Innocentia Hummel and her life here at the convent," Sister Lena told me, "so we thought you might enjoy a behind-the-scenes look at some of our daily duties. We have a very self-sufficient existence

Siessen was originally a Dominican convent, founded in 1260. It was purchased in 1860 by the Franciscan sisters. Right: HUM 88, Heavenly Protection.

here. If we hurry along, we might make it to our first stop just in time." With that said, she turned and led the way down a long, quiet hallway to a stairwell, which, I noticed, was decorated, like the hallway, with collections of handcrafts and artwork.

"These were done by some of our students," Sister Dora said proudly. "Our order works a great deal with children. Even Sister Maria Innocentia, while at the convent, taught art at a secondary school for girls in nearby Saulgau." Sister Lena added, "Often, she would reward the children's good work with a religious picture she had created herself."

As we continued down yet another hallway, the thought crossed my mind that the convent seemed a bit like a small town. Behind one windowed door, I could see the kitchen, where several sisters were gathered around a giant pot of boiling water, making a Swabian specialty, *Spätzle* noodles. Soon after, I passed another door, without a window, labeled *Molkerei* (dairy), and it wasn't long thereafter that my nose detected the first aromatic hints of our destination—the bakery, just as the bread was ready to come out of the oven! Not wanting to disrupt the flurry of activity, I stood quietly on one side of the room as loaf after delicious golden loaf of fresh-baked bread was removed from a large oven, to be replaced by yet another group of doughy hopefuls already sitting on a counter, waiting for their turn in the toasty warmth. In another corner of the room, meanwhile, there was an added buzz of commotion as some other sisters occupied themselves with the assembly of several large *Apfel*- and *Zwetschgenkuchen* (apple and plum cakes), care-

The Franciscan nuns at Siessen lead a very self-sufficient existence. Here, they put some finishing touches on apple and plum cakes.

Mornings are always a busy time in the convent bakery, where the flurry of activity is accompanied by wonderful fresh-baked aromas.

fully arranging slices of fruit from the convent's orchards on top of the dough and sprinkling them with sweet sugar and cinnamon.

Watching it all, I was reminded of those days long ago when I helped my grandmother in the kitchen, baking cakes and cookies—never, though, on such a large scale as this! As busy as each of the sisters were, I was struck by their cheery dispositions, their obvious warmth and animation, and, most of all, by their smiling eyes—reminiscent, I thought, of the expressions Sister Maria Innocentia portrayed in her own artwork.

Siessen, which is a mother house and teaching convent, is home to about 450 nuns. This means a lot of ironing in the laundry, below.

From the bakery, it was just a short walk to another important room—the laundry, where we found two sisters engaged in the unenviable task of doing the convent's ironing, stacks of clean, white, freshly pressed clothes next to them. It was at this point that I finally leaned over to Sister Dora to ask, "How many sis-

ters live here at the convent?" The answer was, "about four hundred fifty."

"It was on August 22, 1933, that Berta Hummel was given the habit of the Sisters of the Third Order of St. Francis, and on August 30, 1934, that she took the vows," explained Sister Lena, as she pointed out a black-and-white picture of a smiling Sister Maria Innocentia. "Not many people realize that Sister was not the first in her family to join an order. On her mother's side of the family, she had an aunt and two great aunts who were also sisters."

Sister Maria Innocentia worked in the embroidery department, above, where she designed clerical vestments and altar clothes.

"Here in the convent," Sister Lena continued, as we traversed a maze of long hallways, "Sister Maria Innocentia was artistically responsible for the design of clerical vestments and altar clothes, which were then embroidered by other sisters."

While opening the door to the embroidery department, she said confidently,

"Our convent was well-known then for its impressive embroidery work, and it still is today. Sister Maria Innocentia was promoted to the head of the department after taking her vows, and she introduced a new, more modern style."

One of the sisters, hearing this, briefly looked up from her work and offered, "there are some church banners and vestments bearing Sister Maria Innocentia's designs which are still being used today." As I looked around this bright and inviting room, I noticed

little touches here and there—reminders, perhaps—of Sister Maria Innocentia, who had died of tuberculosis on November 6, 1946, at the young age of thirty-seven. There was a reproduction of one of her religious paintings hanging on a wall, and a postcard with one of her well-known M.I. Hummel drawings taped to a cabinet. It seemed to me as if the spirit of her presence could still be felt.

One of the final stops on my most memorable visit to Siessen was the garden and greenhouse, where the sisters grow their own vegetables and all the flowers used in the convent, its adjoining church and its chapel. Several sisters who take great joy in exercising their "green thumbs" introduced me to the fruits and blooms of their generously given labor and care—there were sweet, red tomatoes, bushels of onions, countless carrots, and the largest, most brilliant basil I've ever seen! I can't forget the rows upon rows of incredibly large and beautiful bell peppers and zucchini. I looked around in amazement and admiration, wondering if, perhaps, the sisters

These sisters at the Siessen convent take great joy in exercising their "green thumbs," growing all of their own vegetables and flowers.

might share with me some of their gardening secrets.

But more than that, as I looked upon each one of their unforgettable faces and their indelible smiles, I found myself thinking back to that moment long ago when, as a child, I first laid my eyes on the intriguing Hummel figurines in the china cabinet at my friend's house. Now, years later, after spending these past months in Bavaria, and this most remarkable day at the Siessen convent, I not only have a better

understanding of my grand-mother's Bavaria and its people, but I have also seen, with my own eyes, the inspiration for so many of the Hummel figurines. I remember reading that some of Sister Maria Innocentia's loveable images of children as artisans and tradespeople were based on real individuals she knew. It is, I think, a credit to her unmistakable talent and her keen artistic perception that the feelings and emotions expressed in the faces of her endearing compositions are as telling of the period in which they were created as they are of this very moment. They are, as I have found, timeless.

The warm and caring faces of the sisters at Siessen convent remind one of the endearing expressions in Sister Maria Innocentia's own artwork.

Museums of Bavarian Culture

The following museums are just a few of the many dedicated to the preservation of Bavaria's rich past, its unique culture and colorful traditions. We wish to thank the staff of each of these museums for their cooperation and assistance in preparing the photography for this book.

To locate a museum on the map below, check for the corresponding number on the map.

(1) Freilichtmuseum Glentleiten

Bezirk Oberbayern

Dr. Helmut Keim, Museumsdirektor

An der Glentleiten 4, 82439 Grossweil

Tel: 49-8851/185-0, Fax: 49-8851/185-11

e-mail: Freilichtmuseum-Glentleiten@bezirk.oberbayern.de

Internet: http://www.bezirk-oberbayern.de/museen/mus-gle1.html

The museum is open Tuesdays-Sundays from the end of March to the beginning of November, as well as on Mondays that are public holidays. It is open seven days a week in July and August.

Tucked between the Alps and the serene landscapes of the alpine foreland, the open-air museum in Glentleiten provides a unique and historical look at the daily lives, traditions and culture of the people of Oberbayern (Upper Bavaria). Exhibits range from rustic farms and rural homesteads to working forest mills and alpine Almhütten (mountain huts). In addition to original furnishings, workshops and tools, gardens, livestock and regular demonstrations of traditional handicrafts can also be seen. Special exhibits and festivals are held throughout the year. In operation since 1976, the museum is near the towns of Murnau and Kochel am See, north of Garmisch-Partenkirchen.

(2.) Fränkisches Freilandmuseum in Bad Windsheim

Bezirk Mittelfranken

Prof. Dr. Konrad Bedal, Museumsdirektor

Eisweiherweg 1, D-91438 Bad Windsheim

Tel: 49-9841/6680-0, Fax: 49-9841/6680-99

e-mail: info@freilandmuseum.de

Internet: http://www.freilandmuseum.de

The museum is open Tuesdays-Sundays from March through December. It is open seven days a week in June, July and August.

Near Rothenburg ob der Tauber, this open-air museum is devoted to the cultural heritage of the region of Franconia and displays the homes, architectural styles, furnishings, livestock and daily lives of people in the area. An interesting feature is a complex of houses from the Middle Ages. First opened in 1979, the museum comprises more than 70 original buildings exhibited over an area of about 100 acres. Special exhibits, demonstrations and festivals are held throughout the year, bringing to life five centuries of Franconian tradition and culture— from the Nuremberg area and Oberfranken, to Mittlelfranken, Unterfranken and the Altmühl Valley.

(3) Freilichtmuseum Massing

Zweckverband Niederbayerische Freilichtmuseen

Dr. Martin Ortmeier, Museumsleiter

Steinbüchl 5, 84323 Massing

Tel: 49-8724/9603-0, Fax: 49-8724/9603-66

e-mail: massing@freilichtmuseum.de

Internet: http://www.freilichtmuseum.de

The museum is open Tuesdays-Sundays from March through November. It is also open on Mondays that are public holidays.

  The rural reality of everyday farming life in Bavaria's pastoral region of Niederbayern (Lower Bavaria) is the focus of this open-air museum in Massing. Set up in 1969, the museum was one of the first of its kind in Bavaria and it displays a cross-section of regional and historical culture that includes rustic, wooden farmhouses, original furnishings, livestock, orchards and a working hops field. Special exhibitions, demonstrations and festivals are held throughout the year. Massing is located about an hour northeast of Munich, near the town of Altötting.

(4)Heimatmuseum Berchtesgaden

Schloss Adelsheim

Schroffenbergalle 6, 83471 Berchtesgaden

Tel: 49-8652/4410, Fax: 49-8652/948660

The museum is open Tuesdays-Sundays from December-October, and on Mondays that are public holidays. It is closed during the month of November.

  Located in Berchtesgaden's renaissance Adelsheim castle, this museum focuses on the local history, handicrafts, customs and traditions of the people from the region of Berchtesgadener Land. Exhibits include traditional Spanshachtel folk art, antique toys and furniture, folk costumes, and traditional beeswax votives. The museum complex is also home to the workshops of the *Berchtesgadener Handwerkskunst*, where the region's centuries'-old tradition of wooden handicrafts is still kept alive. The unique and colorful folk art created in the workshops is sold at the museum.

Acknowledgements

We are grateful to all who have helped in the preparation of this book, and in particular to the following.

The sisters at Kongregation der Franziskanerinnen von Siessen, Saulgau

The sisters at Missions-Dominikanerinnen, Schlehdorf am Kochelsee

The tourist offices of Bavaria

Bärbel Adelsberger

Martin Berghofer (Schmied)

Monica Baumgartner (Spanschachtelmalerin)

Josef Heinrich (Kaminkehrer)

Alois Höger (Holzbildhauer)

Anton Korber (Kaminkehrer)

Dominikus Miller (Schäffler/Wagner)

Nancy Neumüller

Rudolf Perner GmbH & Co., Glockengiesserei, Passau

Fritz Pfenninger (Schäfer)

Konrad Saal (Holzschnitzer)

Ingrid Sand

Thomas Scheuerer

Franz Stangassinger and Franz Stangassinger, Jr. (Lederhosenmacher)

Maria Valch (Lederhosenmacher-Assistant)

Claudia Willeitner (Gamsbartbinderin)

"Wirtshaus am Freilandmuseum," Bad Windsheim

Walberga Zörner & Family (Almabtrieb)

Goebel of North America, in particular Ken LeFevre and Robert Martin

W. Goebel Porzellanfabrik, in particular Herbert Hennig, Antje Küchle and Dieter Schneider

Ars AG., in particular Brigitte Baüer and Ude Mühletaler

Pedone & Partners, in particular Mike Pedone

Our thanks go to Martin Lederman for his production work on this book.

Photo Credits

We are also grateful to the following for providing additional photography:

Ingrid Grossmann (page 97, bottom, Schäfflertanz; page 114, top, Karfreitag)

H. Keitel (page 59, bottom, Leonhardiritt in Hundham)

Studio Orbivision Christian Prager, Piding (page 58, top, Bad Füssinger, Leonhardiritt)

Marton Radkai (page 58, bottom, Leonhardiritt in Inchenhofen)

Kathleen Saal (page 78, top; page 92, top; page 105, top; page 107, top; page 117, both photos; page 129, top; page 130, top)

Städtische Kurverwaltung, Bad Tölzer (page 59, top, Tölzer Leonardifahrt; page 63, top, Tölzer Weilinachtsmarkt)

Kurverwaltung Garmisch-Partenkirchen (page 60, bottom, Ort mit Eiszapfen; page 61, top, Wanderer im Schnee mit Alpspitze; pages 74-75, Winterpanorama vom Wank aus; page 92, bottom, Faschingszeit)

Tourismusgemeinschaft Inn-Salzach e. V. (page 62, top, Christkindlmarkt, Altötting; page 116 bottom, Maibaumaufstellen Feichten; page 122, Fusswallfahrt nach Altötting; page 127, bottom, Fronleichnams Prozession Altötting)

Fremdenverkehrsamt München (page 62, bottom, Christkindlmarkt München, Fritz Witzig; page 64, Christkindlmarkt München, Heinz Gebhardt; page 65, Christkindlmarkt München, Christl Reiter)

Kurdirektion des Berchtesgadener Landes (page 67, Buttnmandlaufen im Berchtesgadener Land)

Fremdenverkehrsverband Franken e. V. (pages 82-83, Lichterfest Pottenstein; page 115, Osterbrunnen in Pottenstein; page 123, Fronleichnamsprozession in Effeltrich)

Kurverwaltung Mittenwald (page 90, bottom, Maschkera)

Gemeinde Oberammergau (page 138, center, Passionsspiele, Einzug in Jerusalem)

Verein "die Förderer" e.V., Landshuter Hochzeit 1475 (page 139, top, Empfang der Braut auf dem Festplatz)

Index To The Figurines

Following is an index to all of the Hummel figurines shown in this book

HUM 23, Adoration	125	
HUM 261, Angel Duet	79	
HUM 566, Angler, The	128	
HUM 142, Apple Tree Boy	18	
HUM 304, Artist, The	49	
HUM 363, Big Housecleaning	37	
HUM 390, Boy with Accordion	30, cover	
HUM 8, Book Worm	18	
HUM 328, Carnival	93	
HUM 301, Christmas Angel	60, 77	
HUM 2014, Christmas Delivery	61	
HUM 343, Christmas Song	60, 77	
HUM 12, Chimney Sweep	81	
HUM 371, Daddy's Girls	cover	
HUM 495, Evening Prayer	57	
HUM 344, Feathered Friends	129	
HUM 199, Feeding Time	38	
HUM 366, Flying Angel	73	
HUM 369, Follow the Leader	138	
HUM 183, Forest Shrine	125	
HUM 87, For Father	131	
HUM 47, Goose Girl	41	
HUM 150, Happy Days	30	
HUM 88, Heavenly Protection	147	
HUM 312, Honey Lover	39, cover	
HUM 334, Homeward Bound	46	
HUM 459, In the Meadow	128, 129	
HUM 112, Just Resting	34	
HUM 467, Kindergartner, The	27	
HUM 340, Letter to Santa Claus	76	
HUM 89, Little Cellist	6	
HUM 240, Little Drummer	106	
HUM 74, Little Gardener	37, 153	
HUM 200, Little Goat Herder	2	
HUM 73, Little Helper	36	
HUM 80, Little Scholar	27	

HUM 171, Little Sweeper	37	
HUM 308, Little Tailor	101	
HUM 226, Mail is Here, The	121	
HUM 2002, Making New Friends	61	
HUM 342, Mischief Maker	95	
HUM 315, Mountaineer	53	
HUM 214, Nativity Set	72, 73	
HUM 350, On Holiday	113	
HUM 616, Parade of Lights	93	
HUM 800, Proud Moments	cover	
HUM 201, Retreat to Safety	94, 95	
HUM 396, Ride Into Christmas	76	
HUM 348, Ring Around the Rosie	118, back cover	
HUM 55, Saint George	114	
HUM 170, School Boys	26	
HUM 177, School Girls	27	
HUM 82, School Boy	27	
HUM 395, Shepherd Boy	145	
HUM 457, Sound the Trumpet	61	
HUM 353, Spring Dance	51, 94	
HUM 2012, St. Nicholas Day	66	
HUM 255, Stitch in Time, A	135	
HUM 71, Stormy Weather	26	
HUM 131, Street Singer	6	
HUM 668, Strike Up The Band	63	
HUM 437, Tuba Player	105	
HUM 395, Timid Little Sister	10	
HUM 757, Tuneful Trio, A	6	
HUM 387, Valentine Gift	19	
HUM 382, Visiting An Invalid	12	
HUM 154, Waiter	8	
HUM 321, Wash Day	36	
HUM 194, Watchful Angel	60, 77	
HUM 28, Wayside Devotion	124	
HUM 204, Weary Wanderer	12	
HUM 476, Winter Song	61	
HUM 84, Worship	124	